Dealers in HOPE

How to Lead Change and Shape Culture

Robert Mattox M.S.F

"Faith, hope and love abide, wrote the Apostle Paul, but it seems that faith and love get all the attention. Rob Mattox has addressed this lack of focus with an incredible analysis of the hope imperative. He takes the reader from the popular concepts of hope to a deeper appreciation of the necessity of this virtue in our lives, and indeed, in society in general. Rob Mattox made me recognize that I had a huge deficiency in my understanding of this critical issue. The brilliance of his thesis is that he not only defines and expands our understanding of hope, he also provides a template for application of the key principles. This book is long overdue!"

LARRY STOUT, Author of
IDEAL LEADERSHIP:TIME FOR A CHANGE
Shaped a post-communist culture in Latvia, Europe.

"Rob and I have been walking with the Lord together since the summer of 1988 when we were just teenagers. Though we've ministered in different parts of the world over the last twenty years, he has continued to be a source of encouragement and hope for me. When I am confused or discouraged Rob is the first person I call. His depth of study and thought on the topic of hope combined with his degrees and hands-on training in spiritual leadership make him the perfect candidate to write such a book."

JUSTIN CHRISTOPHER, Author of
CAMPUS RENEWAL
Leading a people movement at University of Texas

Dedication

To my daughter Hope. I named you before you were born, before I knew you were a girl, before I knew what tremendous joy you would bring to our lives.

Inspiration

It all began over ten years ago when I read what the Apostle Paul said: "Suffering produces perseverance; perseverance, character; and character, hope."
Romans 5:3-5

I always wondered why hope was at the end of it all.
Now I know.

Table
of Contents

Introduction

Part 1 Hope Changes Reality

Part 2 Dealers in Hope

Appendix

Introduction

We all want to be successful, or at least satisfied when we finish a hard days work. Some people are even ambitious enough to pursue a leadership position and assume responsibility for the success of others. Too often, though, those being led do not feel like the leader has their success in mind. So, they dig their heels into the ground and refuse to move or support the change a leader initiates.

Many leaders fail to lead change or shape culture because they are working in an environment hostile to change. No matter how skilled or naturally talented a person is as a leader, sometimes people refuse to embrace change. They prefer the status quo and this essentially puts a leader out of a job. Leaders make changes, harness change, and manage change, but they do not manage the status quo. That is what managers do.

If your passion is to lead change or shape culture, or this responsibility has been thrust upon you, this book will help you succeed. Successful leaders create hopescapes, environments where significant change emerges. This goes beyond implementing best business practices, mastering the laws of leadership or tweaking self-help techniques. You must become a "dealer in hope."

1 We the People

Dealers In Hope

How did Barack Obama become the first black President of the United States? What enabled Steve Jobs of Apple Inc. to set the pace in the digital entertainment industry? What draws 11 million people to gather online in the virtual world created by Mike Morhaime, CEO and co-founder of Blizzard Inc.? Ultimately, why do some leaders succeed to lead change and shape culture while others fail? It is never just one thing, but there is something powerful enough to not only tip the scale for such leaders but also enable them to harness change and exploit opportunities that others never saw coming. Whether consciously or not, these leaders tapped into what I identify as the hope phenomenon.

Napoleon Bonaparte remarked that a "leader is a dealer in hope." In that spirit, Napoleon fought to institutionalize the French Revolution and permanently establish equality, centralized government and religious tolerance. Napoleon, essentially a man of the people, promised to embody the new values of the culture, end the chaos of the revolution, and fulfill the desperate hopes of the common people.

Unfortunately, in an effort to implement their ideals, Napoleon resorted to tyranny instead of solidarity; hope gave way to fear. He indeed pursued the great dictum of any revolution, that no one is free unless everyone is free, but Napoleon chose military expansion to manage change and stay in control. The General challenged the status quo and initially the people loved him for it, but there is a limit to how much change people can absorb. It seems that control, increased security, and limited privacy, are often the paradoxical price of freedom; inevitably the price becomes too much to pay and leaders' heads roll. A leader's success can therefore be short-lived.

"The times they are a-changing," sang Steve Jobs at the twilight of his first employment with Apple Inc, just a year before he was fired. Supposedly he had too much vision. Similarly, the newly elected British government ousted their hero, Winston Churchill, near the end of the Second World War. And the people eventually grew tired of Napoleon Bonaparte. When people want change, the first person they look to is a leader. When they prefer the status quo, the leader is the first person they seek to get rid of. The leader's dilemma is twofold: to know when the people are ready for change, and what change to make.

Change

There is a greater challenge for those visionary leaders who understand that change itself is upon them and their organization. Daunting is the task to lead and harness the change which the majority of the people do not so keenly perceive or understand. Leaders have to convince the mice that the cheese will one day move, and likely sooner than later. This could mean missing out on crumbs that are there today.

Most people do not perceive change. They do not want it so they do not look for it. Leaders, on the other hand, are wired to notice which way the wind blows and they seize the opportunities which change affords. Sometimes they even create change in order to broaden the choices in hope of more favorable options. Leaders must then open up and illuminate the possibilities to motivate followers who will stand to gain from change. This is the art of dealing in hope. As Kierkegaard said, hope is "passion for the possible," and this passion is powerful. However, people can be very wary of the "possible".

If a leader remains in control and pursues unwanted change or they perpetuate the "possible" which only favors the elite who share in power, the people become hopeless. They either unite in revolution or they fall into despair and accustom themselves to the reality that is offered them. These types of people are easily controlled but much less productive than hopeful people. This happened in Cuba when the Soviet Union collapsed.

The U.S.S.R, which greatly bolstered the Cuban economy, had provided a majority of the country's imports. When the iron curtain fell, Cuba entered both an economic depression and a social depression. People lost hope. A friend of mine who lived through this experience informed me that President Fidel Castro actually asked the Christians to hold self-esteem workshops to encourage the people. To the Communist leader's surprise, the people rebounded and thousands of Cubans planted hundreds of house churches. Underground reform continues there to this day even though most people passively accept Castro's reality.

In keeping with the precedence set by the Revolutionary War, citizens of the United States have usually chosen rebellion over despair when they do not favor the change or do not benefit from the status quo. The Declaration of Independence clearly articulates the reasons for the American Revolution against the King of England. It reads, "We hold these truths to be self-evident, that all men are created equal, that they are endowed by their Creator with certain unalienable Rights, that among these are Life, Liberty and the pursuit of Happiness. That to secure these rights, Governments are instituted among Men, deriving their just powers from the consent of the governed, — That whenever any Form of Government becomes destructive of these ends, it is the Right of the People to alter or to abolish it, and to institute new Government." The common expression of hope in these days takes the shape of aggressive reform rather than revolution, but the tone set by the forefathers still makes an echo.

What was their level of commitment to carry out this Declaration, to ensure that their hopes and the hopes of their children found fulfillment? The end of the document reads, "...with a firm reliance on the protection of Divine Providence, we mutually pledge to each other our Lives, our Fortunes, and our sacred Honor." Hope for the triune ideals of Life, Liberty and the Pursuit of Happiness requires this equal level of sacrifice of lives, fortunes, and honor. As I will show, sacrifice augments the power of hope to change reality and hope provides substantial reason to make such sacrifices. As history records, the forefathers sacrificed much and much blood was spilt but the people won their freedom.

This power to change reality is why leaders deal in hope. The ability to lead change or shape culture exists in this very element of inspiring and harnessing the hopes of followers. In an attempt to do this leaders in the business sector develop well thought out incentive systems and try to satisfy particular hopes of key individuals who champion strategic initiatives. Politicians incessantly poll the populous to make sure they give the people the change they want in exchange for their vote on Election Day. Yet, many leaders fail to lead change or shape culture. Why is this?

Leadership Conditions

Tremendous research exists connecting leadership competencies with successful organizational change management. However, despite all the knowledge and skill leaders possess, failure is as common as it ever was in business. Development Dimensions International, a major consulting firm for Fortune 500 Companies, published research that highlights this phenomenon- "1/3 of managers who get promoted to a leadership position fail." Why is this? Obviously the person's competencies warranted a promotion unless politics was at play. Yet, if they fail they are fired and considered incompetent. Shouldn't the one who did the promoting share in the failure too?

A baseball analogy is fitting. Near the end of the game sometimes a relief pitcher is brought in after the starting pitcher has loaded the bases. The pressure is at a maximum and the stakes are high. If the batter hits a homerun, the four runs scored count against both pitchers- three against the starter and one against the relief pitcher. This illustrates my hypothesis- that sometimes leaders are set up for failure. However, if the leader succeeds in those situations, they are praised, adored, and greatly rewarded. Business works like this- either a leader is competent to solve problems or they are benched. So, for the 1/3 that fail- are these competent leaders being promoted by even more incompetent leaders or is something else going on?

Assuming that a promotion is merited, why does a competent leader fail? Before I answer that, let me ask a couple more questions. There is no doubt failing is part of life and learning from failure is essential for an organization's future success. But are companies failing to learn from failure? Are there equally important factors other than a leader's skills that should be considered in effectively leading change? I suggest a more thorough look into the conditions that create the environment for a leaders' success.

Most leadership books, including theories, models, best practices and even scientific methods for precise execution, primarily focus on improving leadership competencies. There is little research and scarce literature, however, on the conditions of leadership which seek to answer how a leader's place, position, period, and the people surrounding them affect the leader's ability to lead. A prominent author on leadership, John Maxwell, suggests that the right idea at the right time will ensure a competent leader's success. So which factors affect the "right time?" We could resort to Maxwell's *21 Irrefutable Laws* or Stephen Covey's 7 Habits perhaps, but these again mostly focus on best practices. A better understanding of leadership conditions is essential without forgetting the former.

Napoleon Bonaparte understood the need for a hope environment to lead change and shape culture. Barack Obama chose this same theme for his campaign, coupled with the idea of change. He further clarified the type of change he was leading with another word, progress. Steve Jobs constantly introduced change, which is expected in the technology sector. His creation of a Mac culture built on hope bewilders Microsoft, the questionable leader of the industry. Similarly, Mike

Morhaime shapes culture in his online world for gamers. These leaders are dealers in hope.

By examining the leadership conditions which surrounded the Prophet Moses, the one famous for leading the Israelites out of Egypt, out of slavery, but who failed to lead the same people into the Promised Land, we realize that competent leaders must have favorable conditions in order to lead. His successor, Joshua, along with a whole new generation, eventually accomplished what Moses could not. This should serve as a wake-up call: Even the best leaders sometimes fail to lead change. When they do succeed against all odds it seems almost magical, which has often been attributed to a mystical power of intuition or luck. They were in the right place at the right time, so to speak.

Leaders perhaps act intuitively, but there is a secret to their success and valuable insight into their failures that takes searching out. They possess a power to move people who don't want to be moved and a perspective that makes experiences meaningful. In the Art of War, Sun Tzu explains that geography and weather are essential conditions to consider for achieving victory. Likewise, the conditions of leadership must be mastered if you want to be successful. The purpose of this book is to introduce the hope phenomenon as a universal framework for leading change and shaping culture.

Hope Environments- Hopescapes

Before I introduce the idea of hope and explain its construct, it is important to understand the dynamic of hope and the soil where it grows. The hope phenomenon has conditions of its own. To give you some idea of how involved this discovery goes, let me describe my experience so far. In an effort to understand the reality of hope, I studied the topic for more than a decade. I recently received a Masters degree in Strategic Foresight with a concentration in hope theory. Applying hope theory and practice to the business sector is quite difficult but I believe there is a hopescape to be found on Wall Street and Main Street.

Hope is mostly undiscovered country and often a touchy subject. Science has mostly avoided acknowledging hope because of hope's usual religious affiliation and its metaphysical properties which are difficult to quantify. In other words, hope is difficult to get our hands around. Thankfully, one brave scientist and medical physician, Dr. Groopman, spoke up and wrote the *Anatomy of Hope,* which reveals how hope affects cancer patients. He concludes that hopeful people are healthier people, a statement more easily accepted by the softer sciences who have invested considerable research in the subject.

Positive psychology has emerged as a new branch of human science and includes the study of hope theory and practice. Sociology and Philosophy professors are discussing the phenomenon of hope as well. Yet business trends reveal that companies integrate proven scientific theories more than warm-fuzzy ideas like hope. Interestingly, two gurus of business leadership, Kouzes and Pozner, devote one chapter to sustaining hope in their book Credibility: How Leaders Gain and Lose It. But the hope dynamic remains otherwise scarce in business literature. Hype, however, disguised as hope, is widely accepted in marketing business practices.

Hype is the evil twin brother of hope and is often associated with charismatic leaders who greatly inspire their followers. The difference plays out in the end, where "progress" is judged. In tandem, clever marketing usually falls under hype. Yet, with a touch of authenticity, branding and advertisements can capture people's hearts with hope. When marketing is base, hope is reduced to simple desire- lust, envy, narcissism, and greed. Though these remain powerful forces, hope trumps them all.

(Product) RED

In 2006 a capitalistic-humanitarian initiative launched called **(Product) RED**. This is a joint corporate program that donates a portion of the profits on selected items to a Global Fund including World Vision and Habitat for Humanity. Initially GAP clothing advertised one product line with a humorous yet awkwardly offensive slogan: "My narcissism gone global." That was a slap in the face, but at least it was honest and consumers knew that some of their money would help underprivileged people. Now, since the program has matured, the tag line is more positive: "Be part of the solution." Partnering with people and sharing their resources is more powerful than using people with their permission to launder funds for good causes.

Hope is a partnership that exists when vision and values are shared. The dynamics of this relationship between the leader and the followers are founded on trust. Hopescapes exist where trust thrives. When the people know that the leader has their best interests at heart and will strive with them for the mutual good, hope flourishes. Caution: This is different from utilitarianism, which justifies those actions that provide the most good to the most people (usually the "important" people who actually vote). It is also different from "I'll scratch your back if you scratch mine" found in abusive transactional relationships.

Hope thrives in symbiont relationships where destinies are shared. There must be a covenant, a commitment between people who pledge "their lives, their fortunes, their sacred honor" for a common cause. In philosophy this relationship is called "I-Thou" as opposed to I-It. Science is accused of the latter for its objectivity of all phenomena, for treating people like things. Such early scientific approaches to management and leadership saw hope break down when people were considered as "It." An example of this is when consultants measured worker productivity in order to maximize effectiveness.

Companies viewed men as machines and gave them quotas to fill. Monotony replaced creativity and technology replaced humanity. Still today, "Check your brain at the door" is the work place reality for many employees in the world. Unfortunately, in U.S. history, many leaders failed to develop I-Thou relationships with workers and Unions eventually formed. Interestingly, Union is a most appropriate word, which also keeps with U.S. historical precedence.

The preamble of the U.S. Constitution begins, "We the people of the United States, in order to form a more perfect Union..." The forefathers who wrote the document realized that one individual's interests were not as powerful to change the course of history as a common hope shared by a united people. The document expresses even more audacious hopes which intend to usurp the status quo, in order to "...establish Justice, insure domestic Tranquility, provide for the common defence, promote the general Welfare, and secure the Blessings of Liberty to ourselves and our Posterity..." Notice that this hopescape language often makes use of the word "we" and "our." This reveals that hope requires a social context to fulfill its potential.

Not only does the hope dynamic work in the context of a group of people within an organization better than in the isolation of individualism; it thrives where multiple generations are concerned. A Fortune 500 company is likely to consist of these sprawled demographics. If the organizational culture values the skills and strengths that each generation contributes, hope can flourish there. When each generation decides to build on the work of the previous generation, to transcend yet include what came before, hope will experience compounding growth. Yet amidst such potential, hope is surprisingly scarce on Wall Street.

Almost everyone experiences hope on a daily basis, or something they would define as optimism or positive expectation. So if hope seems so common, what is so amazing about exploring hope in a business context? Think about this for a minute: You probably realize when you feel hopeful or when you are sliding into despair; this is emotional intelligence, but how do you conjure inspiration?

Written in the Delphi temple was the aphorism "Know Thyself." This self-awareness usually happens around age 10, when humans develop abstract thinking. For example, Decartes' revelation, "I think therefore I am," would not have been said by most 8 year olds, whose deepest thoughts consists of "I'm bored, therefore I play." So, since you possess the ability to know what you're feeling, why is it so difficult to change the way you feel? Why isn't everyone walking around hopeful and joyful at work? Why can't you grow a hopescape wherever you are?

People do not realize why they do not have hope, only that they lack inspiration. They may have learned that a piece of chocolate can change their mood or that a good book and a hot cup of coffee offer a fresh perspective, but despair still lurks around many corners. Most

11

leaders may be self-motivated and find ways to at least fake it until they make it, but they experience down times too. I encourage you to look beyond ways to cope and persevere to create environments for hope.

Micro & Macro Hopes

According to C.R. Snyder in his work, Psychology of Hope, high-hope people have strong willpower, waypower, and clear goals. Willpower is desire or passion. Waypower is the ability to plan and see pathways to achieve the goal. And high-hope people work to list and clarify their goals continually. Does this sound like you? If you are such a leader who takes initiative and possesses high-hope, you might ask, "How do I inspire hope in others?" "How do I build and sustain momentum to carry the change to completion?" At a macro level, dealers in hope might be asking, "How do I leverage change in this complex political system?" "How do I shape the culture where I work?" "How do I change the world?"

At a micro level, leaders must initiate change all the time. Some changes, though, are as simple as redirecting traffic in a retail store or altering employee work schedules. This type of change does not require hope. However, when a manager asks a department to work overtime for an extended duration with no compensation, this change requires hope. These are difficult economic times and people are being asked to make such sacrifices.

A friend of mine who is a certified black belt in Six Sigma management methodology just received a promotion. He now oversees 150 people but he has been asked to forgo the $30,000 salary increase the position paid the previous supervisor. It's logical to assume that he would accept this promotion out of fear of losing his job. I can attest to the contrary. For some reason, which I will discuss later, my friend holds onto hope even in dark times. He is like Ishmael in Moby Dick who proclaimed, "But I am one of those who never take on about princely fortunes, and am quite content if the world is ready to board and lodge me, while I am putting up at this grim sign of the Thunder Cloud." My friend accepted the promotion because he has hope to lead his company out of the economic storm.

Some dealers in hope are thinking on a macro level and desire to catalyze transformational change. The economic crisis serves as a time to reflect on the results of capitalism, democracy, and the idea of "Progress." I performed a causal layered analysis, a critical thinking framework developed by the professional futurist Sohail Inayatullah, for a local bank where I live. I researched the sub-prime lending practices which led to the credit crisis that spread like an airborne epidemic across all sectors of the global economy. In the discussion I questioned the given assumptions of how the world works. Rarely do financiers and bankers consider the deeper issues behind systemic failures or question the validity of capitalism.

A majority of the world has already concluded that Communism does not work. What other alternative is there? We surely cannot go back to the bartering system. I reflected on the words of Budd Foxx's father in the movie Wall Street, "Create instead of living off the buying and selling of others." This is where I believe capitalism has failed. The Financial market has eclipsed the real market and removed people from the act of creation, from the act of hope.

Until now Progress, the free market, and growth went largely unchecked. Observe closely, though, and you will see that society is now shaping the business culture. "Green technology," "Environmental footprint," and "Sustainable growth," are relatively new values adopted by the business community in an effort to satisfy the conscience of their consumers. Still, intellectuals have rejected the idea of Progress in a reaction against greed and argue that imperialism and colonialism are as strong as ever, if not worse.

It seems to many there is globalization without global concern. Business is leading the way. Some U.S. based companies outsource to China where labor is cheaper. However, as regulation imposes a minimum wage and other protective measures for national workers, companies are looking elsewhere. Some Fortune 500 Companies are researching whether abandoning China and outsourcing rather to Vietnam would be more profitable, given the restrictive government regulations in China. These are survival tactics to increase profit margins. Some would argue that it is practically impossible for companies to stay competitive without pursuing these relocation strategies. Increasing the ROI for stakeholders is the main concern. However, there are some who look for more sustainable business models and ways to implement more conscientious business practices.

I am proud to mention that in my hometown of Williamsport a major health provider and the city officials have cooperated to make business sustainable and still profitable. Susquehanna Health has made some sacrifices to contract local businesses instead of outsourcing to larger national companies and the City has sacrificed to build a highway directly into the hospital campus. The community backs the partnership and has donated millions of dollars to Susquehanna Health's campaign drive. Everyone wins when there is an I-Thou relationship, when there is a shared destiny. This macro-level hope reality serves as an example of doing things differently. It is not business as usual.

Are you thinking about neo-capitalism where business is about something more than meeting the bottom-line? Do you value giving back to the local community where your company operates? If you are a leader faced with the responsibility of changing the course of your organization or shaping its cultural values, or you are assuming it none-the-less, you must become a dealer in hope.

Perhaps you were an idealist but have become jaded in politics now that you have seen more than you would have liked. Now a realist, perhaps you view democracy as a euphemism for despotism. Do you refuse to claim the moral high ground now that torture is justified? Does nationalism and patriotism look more like imperialism lately? I am often frustrated by the fog of politics, especially when people suffer because of personal agendas. For instance, I wonder why the U.S. trades with China but not Cuba, both Communist countries? Some of my friends are Cuban and scrape by with monthly rations that would not even satisfy Americans for a week, all the while China thrives from U.S. business partnerships. I struggle to hope for change. Perhaps you have concluded that politics is not the way to change the world. What else is there?

Some disheartened leaders, fed up with political games, chose military might to overthrow their government because they considered the political system too slow or too corrupt to bring about necessary change. Many people still wonder if peaceful resistance takes too long. African Americans should have enjoyed the "unalienable rights" decades before the 20th Century. It is a marvel that Martin Luther King, Jr. chose reformation over revolution, love over hate, hope over despair.

Revolution or Reformation

A revolution is an overthrow of power. History reveals, though, as in the novel Los de Abajo, a story about the Mexican Revolution, that the new leaders who assume power after a revolution often become what they hated or even worse. Reformation is just as powerful but takes a different approach to change. (I will discuss incremental versus transformational change in chapter four.)

Dr. James Canton, consultant for Fortune 500 Companies and advisor to the former President of the United States, remarked, "The authentic threat that lies at the heart of terrorism (or we could say revolution) and even more conventional wars, is not the battle over religion, power, or even politics. It is the battle over the ideology of the future-whose idea of the future will dominate the planet." Yet, the idea of the future also stirs hope for change.

Are you thinking about neo-democracy where politics is more than ideology and partisanship? Do you value good ideas from wherever and from whomever they may come? Do you evaluate new ideas within an ethical community and implement valuable ones? Or does an ideology (petrified ideas) control your organization? If you are a leader faced with the responsibility of changing the course of your organization or shaping its cultural values, or you are assuming it none-the-less, you must become a dealer in hope.

Dr. Larry Stout shares an anecdote in his leadership book *Time for a Change* that causes me to ponder what is worth fighting for. "As Alexander the Great was setting out on his conquest of Asia, he inquired into the finances of his followers. To ensure that they would not be troubled over the welfare of their dependents during their absence, he distributed crown estates and revenues among them. When he had thus disposed of nearly all the royal resources, his friend General Perdiccas asked Alexander what he had reserved for himself. **"Hope,"** answered the king. "In that case," said Perdiccas, "we who share in your labors will also take part in your hopes." He then refused the estate allotted to him, and several others of the king's friends did the same."

For me, other people's hopes are worth fighting for. As a professional leadership coach I will joyfully partake in your hopes as well as my own.

Hope is not an easy journey or an easy habit to pick up. In some cases it requires a complete mental shift, a totally new worldview. As life without love is not worth living, so leading without hope is the path of dead men walking. I therefore suggest that the most effective leaders are dealers in hope. In the next few chapters I propose a hope paradigm, a framework for leading change and shaping culture and I promise that if you experiment with hope, you will discover a unique power and perspective for effective and meaningful change.

2 HOPE Phenomenon

First Time Experiences

First time experiences leave such a lasting impression. Do you remember your first kiss, where you were and who it was with? I was on the playground during recess. I was in fifth grade. The girl was taller than me and had short curly hair. When our lips locked I was overcome by a wonderful feeling. My stomach converted into a washing machine which someone better described to me later as butterflies. The kiss was so powerful that immediately afterwards I had to sit down. I was leveled. Unfortunately I found out later that the girl was using me to make her old boyfriend jealous. C'est la vie.

I remember the first time I used a chainsaw to cut down a tree. I carefully read the equipment manual beforehand to make sure I held the saw correctly. I memorized the important diagrams on how to make three precise cuts to fell the tree. I cleared a path for my escape route in case the tree unexpectedly fell my way. My heart pounded as I made the final cut. I felt the lumber's latent power which I knew could crush a human being. As the pillar of wood creaked forward, time seemed to slow. The deafening silence finally broke as tree and earth collided and the ground beneath my feet trembled, thrusting me into the present once again.

Even though I was knocked unconscious in my first car wreck, I can still see in my mind's eye my head being thrown through the glass window.

The first time I shot a gun, a .22, I completely missed the rather large target. Having shot many a cap gun as a kid I thought it would be easy with real bullets. My aim eventually improved and my first shooting with the more powerful .38 proved most satisfying. One bullet created a piece of artwork with a Coke can that I kept as a trophy to decorate my office.

As I go through my first time experiences *power* seems to be the key ingredient for such vivid memories. When we reach the end of our known limitations or discover something new, it is powerful. Our brains create new schemas and work to link our memories to help us make sense of the new experiences and information. I wonder what early life experiences introduced you to the phenomenon of hope?

Maybe you remember euphoric excitement lying in bed as a child eagerly anticipating Christmas morning with hopes of unwrapping all the presents stashed under the tree. Did you sneak downstairs to catch a glimpse of Santa? Maybe you looked forward all year to a special family vacation or daddy-daughter trip. For some, your memories might be dark and somewhat void of hope. My father died when I was six and my mom departed into her own mental world of solitude. She took to wandering in search of purpose and we relocated every few years until I started High School. Yet, I looked forward to something new in those moments, traveling the open roads of Texas as a modern day cowboy. So most of my feelings associated with hope came from moving and discovering new places.

As a child, my most profound experience with hope happened in a barbershop while I was waiting my turn to get a haircut. There was a pornographic magazine on the table in front of me and I innocently picked it up to see why everyone was naked. My mom and grand-mother were with me but I didn't flinch. Surprisingly, my mom didn't grab the magazine out of my hand and storm out of the adult barber-shop. She leaned over my shoulder and whispered that good boys don't look at such things and good boys will be rewarded. In hope that what she said was true, I quickly put the magazine back on the table and wandered around the shop.

Later that day the three of us headed to the mall. I saw this shiny red dirt bike in the display window as we entered the building. On our way out my mom asked if I wanted that bike. I flipped. She told me that it was my reward for being a good boy and putting the magazine down. Hope fulfilled!

Sadly, one thing I never experienced was the power of playing on a solid team; winning a championship, crying together over defeat, sharing rides to games, and making friends with teammates. But if you experienced this, you are probably more hopeful about teamwork than I am. You probably believe that T.E.A.M. means Together Everyone Achieves More. Do not take this for granted because many people believe the opposite; "if you want something done right, do it yourself." In my career I worked for five years with the Lone-Ranger mentality until I discovered the power of teamwork. As a leader it took me awhile to realize the truth in the proverb: "If you want to go fast, go alone. If you want to go far, go with others."

True Power

It is logical to conclude that the type of experiences a person has determines their level of hope when similar situations arise. Dr. Groopman believes, "Our sense of hope or despair is reinforced by direct contact with someone who has either prevailed or perished." So, for some people, hope is very powerful. Yet, there is great competition for power.

Many are convinced that money is the greatest power in their world. If you want something, find the resources to acquire it. Others believe love is more powerful than money. After all, "money can't buy you love." It can buy you sex, which persuades some to believe that sex is the greatest motivational power, since "sex sells." Many elderly men refuse to undergo a surgery that would cure their inconvenient prostate problem simply because erectile dysfunction is a common side effect. They live with constant involuntary urination but they will not live without sex.

Others would be lost without their faith, the thread that keeps their world together. And some would argue that knowledge is the greatest power to change the world. Rarely does hope make the list.

22

Instead of sleeping your way to the top, kissing butt, scratching people's backs to get what you want, or proving that you're smarter than everyone else, consider a greater power of influence. Nelson Mandela ended the apartheid from prison. What was the source of this power? He said, "The curious beauty of African music is that it uplifts even as it tells a sad tale. You may be poor, you may have only a ramshackle house, you may have lost your job, but that song gives you hope." Mandela served as a symbol of hope even in exile. I realize that hope alone does not change the world but without it we are truly powerless.

In the competition for power, how does hope stand up against knowledge? Well, if knowledge is power, then hope is weakness since hope is characterized by uncertainty. Let me argue against hope for a second. Knowing where to dig for oil is better than hoping you're digging in the right spot. Knowing how to perform heart surgery is the power to save lives. Possessing a geological map of the ocean floor is the knowledge a submarine crew needs to navigate. Without knowledge we are sunk. However, there has to be a reason to pursue knowledge and that is why hope trumps knowledge.

Some people know how to make a quilt and others couldn't care less. Most people know that spending more than you make leads to debt and financial slavery, but millions do it anyway. Pascal said, "There is a reason that reason knows not." We are emotional beings, not always logical like Vulcans on Star Trek. Furthermore, knowledge is not contagious and so we teach and set up schools to pass on information and wisdom. Hope, however, is contagious and multiplies and compounds. I would like you to consider that hope is a form of knowing and its power can trump knowledge due to the nature of hope's source.

Hope is rooted in desire. If there is no desire for learning or for change, there will be no action. When hopes are high people feel like anything is possible. However, most people live and act based on fear, which creates doubt and produces a diminishing return on expectations until reality is accepted "as is." This leads to frustration and confusion. As author and psychologist John Eldredge says, "It's like walking into a movie twenty minutes late" and you can never catch on to the story. Without hope, life seems void of purpose, like the TV sitcom Seinfeld, but without the humor. Without desire we are a human shell just going through the motions. The only thing fearful people desire is to not feel afraid anymore whereas hopeful people "live in a rich and expansive horizon of meaning," says Patrick Shade, Professor of Philosophy at Rhodes College.

Truly, we don't want money; we want what money can buy us. Even then we are looking for something deeper, perhaps happiness, significance, appreciation, or respect. We don't want sex; we want what sex offers, be it intimacy, ecstasy, or the means to have children. Hope goes to the core of our desires. Hope connects us to the deepest wants of human experience. Hope is the energy to love and the reason to take a step of faith. Hope makes sense of life by giving it purpose.

It seems that in the twilight years of life people awaken to the idea of leaving a legacy and they want to know that their life counts. Baby Boomers see achievement at work as their legacy. Generation X has rejected this philosophy. They work to live and seek unique experiences or encounters, perhaps extreme in nature. Unfortunately, though, most people give-up on their dreams. Henry David Thoreau commented, "Most men lead lives of quiet desperation and go to the grave with the song still in them." Benjamin Franklin said, "Most men die at age 25 but are not buried until they are 70." I assume he meant that people stop dreaming when they become realists at age 25. William Wallace (Braveheart) spoke, "Every man dies. Not every man really lives." These people accept reality "as is" but hope requires a different perspective, to live "as if." Hope lives "as if" reality can and should be different and better

Unique Perspective

Where is the most unlikely place hope could survive? Perhaps in Auschwitz, the German concentration camp of WWII where 3 million people died, 90% of whom were Jews. One man, Viktor Frankl survived this experience with hope in tact and he went on to write books about humanity's search for meaning, asking What is a meaningful life? What is significant? When everything is stripped from you, why still hope? Frankl, a psychologist by profession, invented Logotherapy, a method to help patients find purpose in life to overcome their problems and despair.

In his search for meaning, Frankl evaluated the business perspective, the focus on the bottom-line, and found it one dimensional and unsatisfying. He added a second dimension to consider fulfillment and despair, a hope continuum more-or-less. See Figure 1A. Frankl discovered that a business person could be extremely successful and still despair. Likewise, someone viewed as a failure could find tremendous fulfillment. He concluded that a person's emotional and mental state of hope depends on the presence of purpose. From personal experience in the concentration camps he observed that without purpose people wasted away.

25

According to Frankl there are three ways to discover meaning in life.
1. create a work or do a deed

     (achievement or accomplishment)

2. experience something or encounter someone

3. possess the right attitude toward unavoidable suffering

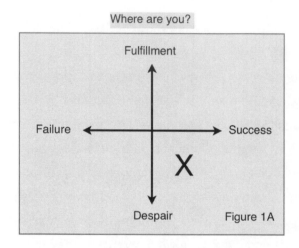

He elaborates more on the second- "...by experiencing something- such as goodness, truth, and beauty- by experiencing nature and culture or, last but not least, by experiencing another human being in his very uniqueness- by loving him." But within the third I believe Frankl stumbles upon the most powerful source of hope- suffering.

It may seem counterintuitive that through suffering humans discover meaning in life. Well, it is the hope perspective that opens up this interpretation. If you read that line quickly, read it again. Not only is hope powerful enough to change the world and shape culture, it is the necessary perspective to discover meaning.

This is shaky ground because many intellectuals today reject, along with Progress, the idea that history is leading to somewhere significant. They view life as ahistorical, without rhyme or reason. Hope is therefore reduced to a means to an end and not allowed to be something that gives meaning to the end or interprets and clarifies the end. This perspective only values hope for practical goal setting and rejects suffering, which seems like an obstacle to hope, as C.R. Snyder states in his Psychology of Hope.

In contrast, Steve Fishman, a professor at the University of North Carolina, interprets the philosopher John Dewey: "We begin to hope, and to employ thinking to reach our goals, only when our habits are interrupted and things go wrong. Thus for Dewey, hope always arises in the context of anxiety and potential despair. Hope is born when we have lost our footing and are struggling to regain our direction." Yet, direction is pointless unless there is a destination. Through suffering we find hope, which orients us when we are lost. Like in a desert, hope is the oasis, not a mirage that deceives our eyes.

Is that not what a leader does, set the direction for the organization and set people's sights on the oasis? Many leaders try to make light of suffering and create a mirage in order to keep hope alive. The paradox is that hope thrives in honest assessment of reality, not in pretend fantasies. Christopher Columbus wrote in his journal, "This day we completely lost sight of land, and many men sighed and wept for fear they would not see it again for a long time. I comforted them with great promises of lands and riches. To sustain their hope and dispel their fears of a long voyage, I decided to reckon fewer leads than we actually made. I did this that they might not think themselves so great a distance from Spain as they really were. For myself, I will keep a confidential accurate reckoning." Though good intentioned, dealers in hope must instead communicate the truth about the situation and rouse the people to find courage and strength to persevere.

Surprisingly, hope is the perspective that makes sense of suffering and interprets trials and failures as significant moments for learning and maturity. In this perspective we discover what we truly want, which is worth the time it takes to unearth. How many organizations have arrived at the exact destination they intended only to realize it was not where they really wanted to be?

How many individuals fought for something and in the end discovered something much more valuable was already in front of them? Sometimes hope helps us see that wanting what we do not have is not as good as wanting what we do have. In this way, the hope perspective can actually help us avoid a lot of unnecessary suffering. It is important that we also avoid taking any shortcuts to realize our hopes because shortcuts surprisingly increase suffering in the long-run. These counter-intuitive realities concerning hope are why defining the phenomenon correctly is so important.

Defining Hope

So, what is hope exactly? Many have chalked it up as wishful thinking and useless to achieve anything. Some say that only lazy people hope things will happen, whereas leaders make things happen. Right? But if Patrick Shade is right, that hope "energizes us," expands our horizon, and enables us to overcome many limitations, we better be sure we don't overlook something we don't understand. Have you ever tried to nail down the hope idea? I must be denser than some because it took me 12 years to develop a working definition and a summarized version for conversation purposes. Consider what great minds have said:

Hope is-

a waking dream- Aristotle

risky imagination- Brueggemann

passion for the possible- Kierkegaard

And from a darker outlook hope is-

a foolish counselor- Plato

a curse upon humanity- Euripides

a human foible that only served to stretch

out suffering- Sophocles

I encourage you to write down your own definition of hope and refer to it later after you finish this book and experiment with the hope framework I propose.

Hope is-

_____

_____

_____

Here is my simple definition-

Hope is orientation and action
towards the most meaningful future.

I will make a few clarifications. This part might seem a little "heady" for a practical leadership book but, as I've heard said, a good teacher makes the complex simple. Let's take a shot at that.

Orientation is about perspective and interpretation. This can be as complex as understanding integrated epistemologies and as strange as contemplating linear versus cyclical time theories. I will not go into depth on these topics in this book but they have been considered in the formation of the definition. Orientation is knowing where you are in relation to other land marks.

Action is a necessary word to highlight because in today's vernacular hope is misunderstood. Even though the ancient Greek word for hope does mean to wait or expect, it is not a passive waiting or wishful thinking. It is an action picture, to hang-on. However, there are times when simply waiting is more difficult than taking action, and a better practice of hope.

Most meaningful means most meaningful. Am I saying that there are some ideas about the future that are better than others? Yes, I believe a world of justice is better than anarchy. On the one hand I appreciate pragmatists who do not ponder Utopian worlds. Yet, like Plato, I do believe there are ideals, or at least better forms than the shadows we now see. There is a matrix and I want out! I guess you could label me as a pragmatic idealist. There, are you happy?

I joke, but some people would discredit this book and chalk me up as an intolerant future fascist. After all, who is to say that a Muslim's view of the future is better than a Marxist's? If you're comfortable with the idea that hope should have moral direction, then you won't mind my clarification of "most meaningful." If you feel otherwise I invite you to continue with this book because I'm sure your hope experiment will teach us both a lot about this phenomenon.

Future can be slightly misleading. I single out this segment of time but I believe the future is only relevant in connection with the past and present. It is one history. However, the future has the potential to bring about what does not yet exist and to offer clarity where the past and present leave us confused. I'm talking about resolution. An event judged as evil when experienced by one generation may later be interpreted as a supreme good which prevented a horrible threat for the future generation. In this way history is judged by all three segments of time. Hope is supremely important to make sense of the past, motivate us in the present, and connect us with the future. The Dutch Sociologist Fred Polak said there is no greater force affecting our present decisions than what we believe about the future.

Psychologists, sociologists, theologians, scientists, and many other professions are deeply interested in the future and its affect on the present. The future is being looked at from these many different perspectives. I have cross-studied each point of view listed and attempted to integrate each domain's understanding of hope. However, literature on a mathematician's analysis of hope would be hard to find as would be the Plumber's Manifesto of Hope. I have not tried to draw conclusions from sectors in society that do not contemplate the phenomenon. To be fair, I have considered many other driving forces that shape the future, which I will discuss in the next chapter.

Perhaps the professions listed would not agree with my aggregate view of hope. This is the first attempt at a holistic framework that I have seen and it is what makes this book unique. You will have to judge for yourself if the hope paradigm is reasonable from the knowledge you possess. I do propose that with such a diverse perspective on the topic, that hope is a construct, not just an element, meaning there are many parts to the whole.

For a business context the hope paradigm consists of six essential elements. Three are effective to initiate change and build momentum and three will create ownership and sustain the momentum for a truly successful and effective change. As I have experienced and learned in my study, hope often functions like a system with positive reinforcing feedback loops. That might sound complicated but it's as simple as a snowball getting bigger and bigger as it rolls down the mountain. Business finance people could relate it to compounding interest. This is what I marvel at most about hope, how an increase in one element can power-up another and work its way back to super-size hope, which is necessary when life keeps throwing bigger obstacles or trials our way. I explain systems thinking and the hope system in the next chapter.

Creating Hopescapes

The first, most important element of hope, is the promise. Without a promise hope absolutely cannot exist. Promises can be explicit or implicit. Implicit promises exist in our memories, like with food. We order what we prefer because sausage promises to be salty, chocolate promises to be sweet, and coffee promises to wake us the hell up. Sometimes a leader doesn't have to say anything to make a promise and within an organization's culture there already exist structures and norms based on promises. Leaders, especially politicians, sometimes make more promises than they can keep, let alone recollect, which can be problematic and cause hope to shut down quickly.

Simply put, people behave in such a way so that they will be rewarded. If they know creative ideas are either stolen or hushed, people will keep their thoughts to themselves. It will be a challenge for leaders to create an innovative atmosphere in such a culture. The leader needs to communicate a new promise and follow up on it immediately. "From now on..." is a great phrase to clarify new values. There is obviously more to it than that, which brings us to element number two- *voice*.

Voices must be heard. Promises from the leader must intersect with the people's unified voice. If individuals and groups are not free to express what they think about the way things are done, without getting reprimanded or marginalized, hope will be squashed. People must feel that their concerns are being heard and considered. However, voice does not necessarily include excuses, complaining, whining, griping, and gossip. Hope will most likely emerge from the Voice that is constructive in its criticism, that offers solutions for problems, and expresses openness to change. Given these parameters, questions should be encouraged, doubts permitted to be verbalized, and complaints collected and qualified.

It is important to realize that many variables affect a person's hope level. sometimes people lack emotional strength or the conversation skills to express their hurts and frustrations in a mature, nonthreatening way. It was never taught to them, perhaps. Others have lived hopeless for years so their comments take a rebellious form. This serves as an outlet for their anger since things they wish would change never do. Some people carry their hopeless disposition with them. Maybe relationships at home are strained or a relative is sick with cancer. Be aware too that their poor communication might be a former leader's fault.

Even though an individual's voice is important, in terms of inspiring hope to lead change, the voice of a unified group is what should be weighed the most. When people realize that leadership takes their concerns and interests to heart, they will be more open to change.

Thirdly, at this point promises and voice intersect to create an atmosphere where imaginations can run wild. Walter Brueggemann, a theologian who wrote numerous books on the subject of hope, defined the practice of hope as risky imagination. People may say they want a leader to promise he or she will do everything for them and take care of them, but this will not create hope. They must participate and imagine the future with you.

The intersection of Voice and Promises help create a hopescape, an environment where hope can flourish. "Fresh solutions will be rewarded," is an open promise that stirs people's imagination. They begin to think creatively about dozens of ways to solve a problem. This is a collaborative process between leaders and followers. For a hopescape to develop, people essentially need to know that the leader will support them, allocate enough resources and time to them to do the work that is imagined, and that everyone will share in the success.

Ghengis Khan- "How to create a hopescape"

The Khans of Mongolia were known for their ruthlessness in dealing with subjects (direct reports you might say). It was common practice that the Khans kept the plunder and gave the scraps to their clan members after battles were won. The Great Khan, Ghengis, started a new precedent, though. He kept ten percent for himself and his warriors were instructed to divide the rest of the spoils equally. This won him great favor and it established a new image for leadership. Ghengis Khan also introduced a brilliant tactic to deal with recently seized cities. He killed all the rulers in power and instituted the poorest people as the local ruling leadership. By upending the status quo and listening to the voice of the people Ghengis won their loyalty. His imagination in battle, social structures and in commerce earned Ghengis Khan a place among those who shaped the modern world.

Imagination pushes through bottlenecks and overcomes the limitations organizations face if it is empowered by promises and by the synergy of a new conversation among the voices. At this stage In leading change the old conversation of "what's wrong with the world" is ending. The elephant in the room has been discussed and energy is redirected towards positive goal setting. Now there is space for new ideas and out-of-the-box thinking. There is more time for creative innovation since people aren't griping at the water cooler every hour.

Consider the hopescapes at Disney, Google, and 3M which thrive on imagination. Google and 3M allow time for their employees to work on pet projects with the hope that innovative creations will emerge. In the era where intellectual property is a company's greatest capital, imagination is essential to the success of any organization.

35

Even IT professionals who write code for the banking industry have to imagine how to improve current systems and then they write out the solution. You might prefer the term creative problem-solving instead of imagination to keep with your organization's culture but the process is the same.

Keep in mind that even though one individual might invent the next gizmo, it takes many departments to get the product or service to the customer. Have you ever stayed in the movie theater until the lights came on at the end of the movie? Hundreds, even thousands of people's names scroll in the credits. We might remember the actors' names but they hardly do a fraction of the work. Imagination alone will not carry you. The next step is teamwork.

In summary: a hopescape is created by combining the **Voice** of the people with the **Promises** of the leaders, releasing **Imaginations** to run wild. Change is initiated in these first three steps. However, momentum must be sustained and it is essential to walk through the whole process if you are to reap the rewards of hope. The next three steps will take you the distance and enable you to finish strong.

Let me first stitch the six steps together so we see the big-picture. I want to share with you a metaphor for hope so that we can better understand how hope grows and becomes powerful enough for transformational change. Forging hope is a high-pressured process like going from a piece of coal to a bright shiny diamond.

3 HOPE Diamonds

Metaphor for Hope

A diamond is a remarkable substance that requires specific conditions in the formation process. Only in a high temperature, high pressure environment deep in the earth's lithospheric mantle can carbon atoms assemble in the isometric-hexoctahedral crystal lattice. If there are slight variations in these conditions, then a diamond will never form. In order for diamonds to be mined they must make the 100-mile journey to the earth's crust. Underground volcanic eruptions deliver the diamonds to the surface as gifts to humans who are captivated by nature's masterpiece. Despite the rare conditions under which diamonds can form and the scarcity in the consumer market, 130 million carats are mined annually. That is 57,000 pounds of rock.

Diamonds have fascinating characteristics. The word diamond means unbreakable or untamed. A diamond's hardness is exploited to drill, cut, polish and grind materials. Some diamonds even conduct electricity. Only the gemstones, though, are valued for their sparkle. As an adornment piece people value diamonds for their *clarity*, *cut*, *color*, and *carat* weight and rate them based on these four categories, otherwise known as the 4 C's.

In order to increase value and boost demand in the gem markets, governments and cartels actually buy-up the diamond supply. It might seem corrupt, but imagine if everyone walked around with two or three diamonds on their hand, then an engagement ring would not possess the power it does as a symbol of promise and commitment.

Unfortunately hope has no cartel to protect its value and everyone thinks they can tap into its power. Thankfully many imitations have been exposed as synthetic cubic zirconia types of hope. The true diamonds, however, are tested and proven, like the Hope Diamond. Named after Henry Philip Hope, this 45 carat blue gem has an interesting history possibly dating back to 1668. Since then it has been sold many times to pay off personal and royal family debts. It was eventually donated to the Smithsonian Institute in Washington D.C. where it currently resides. It has withstood the test of time and the exhibit today is still the most popular in the Natural Science Museum.

Meaning of the Metaphor

The hope paradigm that I am proposing is similar to the diamond formation process. Thus far, suffering has been introduced as the main source from where hope emerges. Adversity could be considered the high-temperature, high-pressure conditions necessary for hope to form. In a business context this means that things aren't going well. Profits are down, morale is low, customers are dissatisfied, competition is stiff, or whatever unpleasant current reality your organization might face.

As a leader you are seeking an alternative future, a way out, new horizons, or a simple solution to a problem that's dogged you for months, maybe years. There is a volcanic eruption, a mix of promises made and voices crying out for things to get better. It might be your boss bringing you into his office and giving you the smack down. It might be a customer giving you an earful. It might be a direct report holding you in contempt.

It is at this point the imagination is mined for valuables and a diamond is discovered. But how do you know it is the Hope diamond? How valuable is it? Like the 4C's to assess a diamond, there are four important elements of the hope diamond- *imagination*, *teamwork*, *risk* and *identity*. I have already discussed imagination but I would like to reiterate that imagination is the result of combining promises with voice. Imagination then combines with these other parts to form the hope system, or hope diamond.

These four parts combine to give the diamond its sparkle. But if all you're after is razzle-dazzle, almost any cubic zirconia will do. If you want something impressive, captivating, breathtaking, and enduring, maybe I can interest you in a hope diamond. By understanding the hope system we can better understand the success of Obama's campaign strategy, the breadth of Steve Jobs digital empire and the attraction to Mike Morhaime's virtual world. I guarantee you that these leaders shine because they are true dealers in authentic hope.

Hope's Sparkle

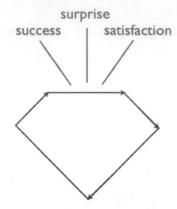

The power of a diamond as a gem rests in its ability to capture light and reflect it into a magnificent spectrum of color. It catches our eye. The unique structure of a diamond effectively obstructs the speed of light and slows it down by 100,000 miles per hour. It can almost grab light and possess it. In my culture the diamond is a powerful gift that can also capture a woman's heart. Girls dream of the day when a handsome young man will get down on one knee, open up a small treasure box, and propose marriage to them. Diamonds are expensive and sometimes they have even greater sentimental value when they are handed down from one generation to the next. When the woman shows off her diamond, people see that it shines and sparkles and excitement fills the room.

The hope paradigm (diamond) sparkles too, if you have authentic hope. There are three fruits of hope that your organization will experience as a result of practicing hope. The first fruit is goal achievement, of course, which we can call **success**. Hope goes beyond this, though, to the point where expectations will be exceeded, which we can call **surprise**. Finally, there will be tremendous joy, which we can call

satisfaction. The end result will be much more meaningful because it will speak of something greater than increased profit margins.

If selling more hamburgers or nails or vacuum cleaners is all you're interested in, then I do not recommend dabbling in hope. Hope is a powerful system, not a quick fix or a plug and play. Here is my warning label: You would probably agree that it is not wise for a man to give a diamond ring to a girl and then start dating other women. Likewise, hope will not suffer being controlled or exploited. The good news is that you can harness its power.

Harnessing Hope
Systems Thinking Approach

Some systems are simple to play with, like the thermostat which controls the electric heat. Everyone feels fairly confident that a slight lift of the switch will successfully manipulate the air temperature. Some people, however, are unaware of how the system works. So, when it gets too hot, they open the window, not realizing that this action kicks on the thermostat which generates even more heat. The leverage point for change is the thermostat, not the window.

Leaders must discover the leverage point for effective change in every situation. Some systems boggle even brilliant minds, like supply and demand for oil. If oil prices shoot up $10 a barrel within a week, who is responsible? The people in my small town would place the blame on greedy oil companies. Some would assume that since OPEC regulates oil production, they must be the leverage point. Or would the war in the Congo or Sudan or Iraq be the reason for a price spike? Sometimes a natural catastrophe like hurricane Katrina, which struck

New Orleans in 2005, can cause the market to jump.

There are many variables in the oil market system which per-plex even the experts. A year ago, in 2008, these experts predicted gas prices in the U.S. to soar from $4 to $8 a gallon. The opposite occurred. This might seem like a problem suited for economists but leaders have to decide whether to expand drilling, retool to build more gasoline effi-cient automobiles, or pursue fuel independence. From thermostats to the oil market, systems thinking is essential for dealers in hope.

A system can be understood as the relationships between the parts that affect the whole, with the understanding that the whole is greater than the sum of the parts. Simply breaking down a problem or a machine into its basic units does not serve well to explain what is really going on. Rather, you could say that systems thinking is a holistic per-spective that appreciates the impact of interconnected variables. Peter Senge, director of the Center for Organizational Learning at the MIT Sloan School of Management, describes systems thinking as the Fifth Discipline, which he illustrates is essential for the learning organization. The opposite of this is linear thinking of cause and effect, which mostly produces a reactionary posture. A dealer in hope must be proactive, not reactive.

Personal Example

I got into a fight one time with a guy named Tom because he assumed I had purposely pushed him from behind. I was in grade school waiting in line in the gym. Someone from behind pushed me and I could not help but collide with the guy in front of me. This really irri-tated Tom and he challenged me to a fight after school at the railroad tracks. He was not interested in my explanation of what truly happened but reacted in anger to what he perceived was the source of the problem.

A view of the whole must be considered for wise decision-making, which is what Tom lacked. The tricky part, though, is the counter intuitive aspect of systems thinking which arises when an improvement in one part of the system can actually have a negative affect on another part. Not surprisingly, leaders often pick a fight before they understand the situation and before they are able to determine the leverage points for effective change. In my story it was to my surprise and to Tom's shame that I walked away the victor at the railroad tracks.

Revolutionary Change

Some leaders are in search of revolutionary change. Brian McLaren, author and Pastor, presents a macro system of the way the world works, which comprises three subsystems: the prosperity system, the security system, and the equity system. In summary, the prosperous desire security to protect their right to pursue happiness. The equity system exists to protect the right for everyone to pursue happiness and prosperity. McLaren continues with the corruption of the systems: unsustainable growth, expanding economic inequality, and violent measures that attempt to restore the balance. Like most revolutionaries, McLaren is searching for something greater than a leverage point; he wants to reset the system.

The title of McLaren's book, "Everything Must Change," presents the solution that the world must embrace a new framing story. This is similar to Peter Senge's concept of mental models (Second Discipline for learning organizations) and on track with Thomas Kuhn's revolutionary idea of paradigm shifts. A framing story is basically a worldview and a systems perspective that recognizes how the main characters work together. It is important to keep in mind, however, that there are different types of systems.

Open & Closed Systems

An open system is defined as a system which interacts and adapts to the environment. One of the reasons most people lose heart so easily or are inclined to despair is because they treat hope like a closed system. Hope is not a formula, in that people cannot set whatever goal they desire and expect things to turn out exactly as they envisioned and planned. Some type-A leaders would disagree and argue against compromising tactics or veering from the objective. They believe that once a goal is set, it must be achieved. But just because you can doesn't mean you should. The green technology movement is a reactive solution to the "successful" goal achievement that did not consider the environment i.e., "Progress" is slowly destroying our world.

Batman's Best Business Practices

In the movie Batman Begins, Bruce Wayne seeks the means to fight injustice. His mentor, Ra's al Ghul, takes him to a frozen lake to learn martial arts on ice. Empowered by his anger, the nascent swordsman Bruce Wayne pins his opponent. Ra's al Ghul rebukes his protegé, "You haven't beaten me. You have sacrificed sure footing for a killing stroke," and he taps the ice. The lake breaks open and Bruce falls into the freezing cold water. The lesson- "mind your surroundings."

Business leaders need to learn what the Billionaire Bruce Wayne learned. Many have already discovered that, now more than ever, change is upon them. They must adapt. The key is not to react but to harness change.

Emergent Properties

Academicians are applying cutting-edge research on complex adaptive systems theory to the business world in the context of decentralized organizational management. They have found that the advantages to working with change from an adaptive posture are even broader than efficiency in relationship functionality. This flexible approach to work and change allows for creation. In *Harnessing Complexity,* Robert Axelrod and Michael Cohen explain the phenomenon that results in "...emergent properties, which are properties of the system that the separate parts do not have. For example, no single neuron has consciousness, but the human brain does have consciousness as an emergent property." It's like a combo meal at any fast food restaurant. Buying all the items separately costs "X" amount of dollars, but when you buy them together, the price magically drops.

Understanding emergent properties leads to increased innovation. Creation is termed innovation in the business community but there is misrepresentation in this variation. Invention means to create something new. Innovation means having the capacity to reproduce the invention successfully and profitably. Many tremendous inventions have been sidelined because they were too expensive to manufacture on a grand scale. Hydrogen, the most plentiful substance in the Universe, could be used to fuel automobiles; however, the estimates to harness that energy right now would put a car between $300,000 to $1,000,000. That is a 30 year mortgage at $2K a month. Businesses are interested in innovation, not inventions per se, but these two go hand-in-hand. A system that adapts to the environment and harnesses the complexity of change experiences both in the miracle of emergent properties.

Hope is an Open System

Hope functions like an open system and is constantly adapting to the imminent future in expectation of change. It is a flexible structure that allows for constant capacity expansion in order to make room for new creations. Hope therefore embraces shifting strategies and new identities, yet most dying companies and immature leadership styles still prefer control and predictability. Be aware, that even in the area of financial sales forecasting, analysts only possess the illusion of certainty. Incremental change might be calculated but more significant transformational change is usually not factored in. What these leaders see is a mirage in the dessert, not the oasis. Hope is in motion, not stagnant. It is open to the future, not closed.

Fast Food Folly

Why do fast food restaurants mostly employ teenagers and individuals with minimum education and experience high turnover? They are centralized organizations that function like closed systems and they try to control almost everything. They spawn hopeless environments that most people consider a temporary employment solution until they can find something better. However, if you insert hope in the same organization, the environment becomes quite different.

46

Truett Cathy of Chick-fil-A developed a fast food chain of over 1000 restaurants and his success is also satisfying because he has a broader perspective than the one-dimensional bottom-line. Cathy understands that humans are meant to thrive, not just survive. Acting on this belief, the company offers college scholarship programs and professional development for their employees. Cathy also knows that life is a balance of work and rest. All the stores are closed on Sundays to give his employees time to rejuvenate. Yet, when it comes to work, Cathy appreciates the self-sacrifice aspect of hope. When economic times were tough, Cathy made sacrifices so others would not have to. "I didn't take a salary that year because I didn't want our employees to take pay cuts. I struggled with this but I was determined not to lose sleep over it."

When inflation hit in 1974 the cost to open a single Chick-fil-A increased by $25,000. Like many business owners, Cathy put his personal property assets on the line as collateral to borrow the $600,000 necessary to open fourteen stores that year. In contrast, many CEOs today have little invested in the company they run. Essentially organizations hire these leaders to manage what does not belong to them. This is a poor practice of hope. The forefathers wrote, "We pledge our fortunes" and Cathy echoes this principle: "Too many CEOs are leaving sinking ships. They should be the last ones to leave the company. If some people are losing money, everyone should lose money, not just the stockholders." Many CEO's will become successful and rich but their legacy will disappoint because they do not inspire hope. They "get theirs" and they get out. Dealers in hope do not profit from the loss of others; they create abundance for many.

This abundance comes from practicing hope as an open system. How does that work? The process develops like this- as people **imagine** together, they see the value and necessity of **teamwork**. When they begin to work towards a goal they will most definitely encounter obstacles. They must **take risks** to achieve their goal. This may require failure and disappointment. Most efforts end here unless people **identify** with the greatness of the organization and with those who sacrificed and went before them. The process actually swells as it progresses, as in a reinforcing feedback loop. As imagination increases, team work increases. As team work increases the need for risk taking to achieve greater goals increases. As risk taking increases, identity is strengthened. And as identity crystalizes, hope increases. This hope in turn increases every other single element in the hope diamond and the feedback becomes incredibly powerful.

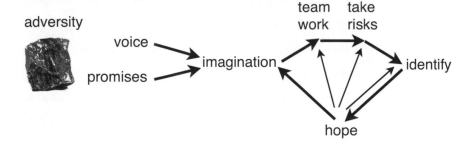

There are two major things to note-

1. *Risk taking* is not recklessness, but calculated action and absolutely necessary to achieve the goal. Hope truly increases courage and wisdom to take risks, rather than promote risky behavior.

2. *Identity* must form in the context of a story. People who love where they work usually identify with the organization's values. Values are simply ideas that people like. But the story is what assigns value to the idea.

Senge would say compliance becomes commitment where there are shared values. However, values alone are not enough to hold and maintain the momentum for change. For example, "Grit your teeth and bear it," may temporarily inspire people to be "hard core," to fulfill their duty (a value of the WWII generation), but relying on values will not sustain hope.

In Steven Spielberg's Band of Brothers the elite paratroopers of WWII face one battle after another and it seems endless. They lose their reason to fight until they stumble across the concentration camps and witness the evil suffering imposed on innocent people. Then and there they remember that they are in the middle of the classic story- good versus evil. The soldiers also realize that, for the prisoners of Auschwitz, the story is all wrong. The soldiers bolster their strength to fight for a better reality. The new clarity of purpose renewed their passion to finish the war!

Values are not enough. People strongly identify with another person's story. It's more than shared values; it's an emotional connection with a character in a story, a story they see unfolding before them.

Character

Character development is the maturation of a person's identity, and there are layers to character. Character is a mark, like a letter. It is also the embodiment of virtues or traits (values) and finally, it is a role in a story. Each touches a progressively deeper level in a person's identity. The mark might be their name, a tattoo, their British accent, or any other distinguishing physical feature. On a deeper level, a person's traits are reflected in their behavior or personality. Deeper still, the role people assume in life is defined by their purpose and their worldview- their belief system and the story they tell themselves. How do you see yourself? What role are you filling?

Levels of Character

Mark- name, tattoo, accent, how someone laughs

Behavior- personality, moodiness, habits

Role- purpose one fulfills- "party animal," "geek," "hero," "soccer-mom"

Character of Hope

In the movie *The Edge*, Anthony Hopkins plays a billionaire who gets lost in the Alaskan wilderness with two other men. A Kodiak bear tracks them and kills one companion. Charles, played by Hopkins, is fed up with trying to outrun the predator. Bob, played by Alec Baldwin, loses hope and gives up on the possibility for survival. Charles decides to become the predator and kill the bear but he first has to convince Bob that it is even possible.

They argue.

Bob: What are we going to use to bait him Charles?

Charles: We lure him in. You know, Masai boys in Africa, eleven years old- they kill lions with spears.

Bob: Uh huh... how do we *lure* him? (sarcastic tone)

Charles: Eleven year old boys kill a lion. Did you know Indian boys used to run up to the bear and slap him, count coup on him as a test of manhood?

Bob: No, Charles. How are **we** going to lure him?

Charles: Blood. (cuts his thumb deeply with a knife). Blood!
Charles strategizes a bit and then concludes. "It can be done."
Do you believe it Bob? Do you believe it?

Bob: I don't know Charles.

Charles: Huh?

Bob: I don't think it will work Charles.

Charles: It will work!

Bob. No!

Charles: It will work. What one man can do, another can do (points knife at Bob).

Bob: We can't kill the bear Charles. He's ahead of us all the time. It's like he's reading our minds. He's stalking us for God's sake!

Charles: You want to die out here. Huh? Then die. But I tell you what. I'm not going to die. I'm not going to die. No, I'm going to kill the bear. Say it, "I'm going to kill the bear." (tosses the knife to Bob). Say it, "I'm going to kill the bear." Say it. Say, "I'm gonna kill the bear." Say it!

Bob: (mutters) I'm gonna kill the bear.

Charles: Say it again!

Bob: (a bit louder) I'm gonna kill the bear.

51

Charles: And again!

Bob: (shouting) I'm gonna kill the bear!

Charles: Good. What one man can do, another can do.

Bob: (emphatically) What one man can do, another can do.

Charles: Say it again!

Bob: What one man can do, another can do!

Charles: And again!

Bob: WHAT ONE MAN CAN DO ANOTHER CAN DO!

Charles: Yeah!

"What one man can do, another can do" is the phrase that invokes identity! But the process starts with imagination. As they look at the picture on the knife box, Charles explains how they can get the bear to fall on a spear and use his own weight to kill him. But it takes team work and they initially encounter failure. Their first attempt with a swinging spiked contraption only slightly wounds the bear, mostly irritating it more. They run and slide down a rocky slope to gain better ground where they have prepared a stronger defense and have access to more spears. Bob risks a jab and the bear swipes at him, sending him flying through the air. Charles makes a stand and fixes one end of his spear against a rock. He leverages the weapon as the bear rears and then falls on the sharp wooden spear. The stick penetrates the entire body as the bear collapses on Charles.

In killing the bear the men become warriors, achieving more than they had expected. While cooking the meat over a fire they reflect on their successful, satisfying and surprising accomplishment, eyes lit with hope's sparkle.

Charles: For all my life, I've wanted to do something that was un-
      equivocal.
Bob: Well, Charlie, I certainly think this qualifies.

Charles decides that when he returns home he will change his
life and Bob comments that he would be the first. For all of his billions of
dollars, the meaning of life had eluded him- until he was tested in the
wilderness and overcame adversity through authentic hope. Both men
find true hope when they walk through the process (the hope system)-
through imagination, teamwork, risk taking and identifying with the
Masai children and Indian boys of long ago. With that hope they are
able to continue on and Charles is eventually rescued.

Unfortunately for Bob, he does not assume his new identity and
when the opportune moment arises, he resorts to his old framing story-
the man who was having an affair with Charles' wife and who planned
to kill him for his money. After finding a rifle at a refuge, Bob holds Charles at gun point and walks him out into the woods to murder him there.
Charles outwits him and leads Bob into a bear trap where he acciden-
tally steps into a deadfall, suffering a fatal wound. This symbolic event
reveals Bob's true identity as the real bear stalking Charles.

Emerging Purpose

One major emergent property evolving from the hope system is
a narrative, a story which creates and defines the participants' purpose
in life. It fills up with main and supporting characters. It develops a plot
drenched in conflict, moves towards a climax, which culminates in resolution, and then picks up again to introduce another story. In this Epic,

the conflict between good and evil is an organization's fight to survive and thrive, against competition, against other external and internal forces. Can you look Change in the eye and determine whether it is friend or foe, good or evil? We must explore the dynamic of change and the forces driving it in order to wield hope in the struggle to lead change and shape culture.

CHANGE

Guns, Germs & Steel

If asked, most people in the United States will say that they have a vivid memory of where they were when President John F. Kennedy was assassinated or when the tragedy of 9/11 occurred. I remember walking into work at the Valley Forge Convention Center, glancing at the TV behind the security guard, and seeing one of the Twin Towers on fire. Three months later my wife and I spent our anniversary in New York City and we stood at Ground Zero amazed by the devastation of the attack. Pictures of lost loved ones covered the walls of the blocked off areas. Rubble was still being moved and stories still being told by locals describing the serendipitous events that prevented them from being in the building that day. In that moment we experienced history as real and tangible.

Except for days like September 11, 2001, we do not appreciate the dramatic events or perceive the subtle shifts that have transformed cultures. Maybe a lingering ethnocentrism blocked me from contemplating the reasons for one destiny altering event- the extinction of a race. I never asked myself why ninety percent of the indigenous people of North America were wiped out by a plague when the Europeans arrived. Why didn't the Europeans contract a deadly disease from the Indians instead?

Jared Diamond wrote a fascinating book, *Guns, Germs and Steel* to answer such a paramount, yet overlooked question in which he weighs the effect of technology, evolution and human ideas against their ability to change the course of history. In this era, technology receives the bulk of the positive press coverage today and is considered the primary driving force of change in our society.

It is obvious that since the 18th Century, the rate of change has increased exponentially due to advances in technology and this trend is not likely to reverse itself. As powerful as technology is, however, few developments have been as disruptive as a culture brought to the brink of extinction by disease. Evolution is a force to be reckoned with. Some would argue, though, that technology's subtle encroachment has transformed culture to such a degree that it could one day destroy humanity too. They fear the near extinction of the human race, as depicted in the blockbuster films, the Matrix, I Robot, and the Terminator series.

Is there any doubt that movies and television have forever changed the communication industry? These technologies have evolved into the internet, an even more powerful and pervasive communication platform which Google is utilizing to make all knowledge available and easily accessible with key-word searches. Soon not only information, but wisdom will be googled, e.g., Doctors and veterinarians already offer medical treatment suggestions online. So, even though some might conclude that technology is driving change, we must ask what is driving technological development. Is it market forces, cultural ideas, or something else?

Everyone wants to look behind the curtain to see if the Wizard of Oz is truly powerful and so I will try to reveal technology's secret, if there is one. If you remember, after the veil was lifted, and the Wizard was revealed as a phony, his reputation did not suffer- simply because he owned a hot air balloon. This device promised to be the technology that would take Dorothy home. Following this metaphor, technology initially seems powerful, like the Wizard, until we figure out how things work. Then technology often seems weak because, in the end, we realize it is only powerful enough to change our behavior but impotent to change our worldview, e.g., texting is a new way to send a message but it doesn't influence our views on abortion or immigration.

It is worth mentioning that the Wizard and his science did not grant Dorothy and her friends any miracles. Instead, he pointed out that they already possessed what they were looking for. So, technology might be flashy, but is it as powerful as courage, a brain full of ideas, or a loving heart? And don't forget about Dorothy's feet, and her sincere wishing, which could take her any place she wanted to go. No hot air balloon could do that for her.

Having said all that, there is a big difference watching the latter half of the film in color, which was made possible by technology. Half the movie is shown in black and white and the other half in color. What is the message there?

Marshall McLuhan, educator and philosopher, coined the phrase the "medium is the message," which explains that technology could shape the way people think even beyond the content presented. For example, the mere presence of a television set turned on in the kitchen communicates a message. At prime-time, this medium presents extreme, violent crimes in the context of a family dinner, neutralizing the traumatic and making the extraordinary commonplace. So, it is plausible that the nature of this medium could increase social tolerance of violence. Have we invited news reporters in the TV set to the kitchen table and are they now considered experts whose knowledge trumps parental authority?

This strange voice at the dinner table subtly determines the topic of conversation, granting the TV control. This means that the Wizard of Oz has sealed himself in and there is no way to look behind the curtain. Not only this, but conversation is reduced to commentary with no invitation for response. The media controls what information and how much information is shared. This was the case until 2006 when "bloggers" won Time Magazine's Person of the Year and the voice of the average person was heard once again.

This new trend took off in 2008-2009, empowered by technology's latest innovation- social networking. Websites like Facebook and Twitter exist as forums for common people to control information and due to their popularity, the mass media networks have had to embrace their influence. Commentary has finally evolved into conversation after a long century of monopolized mainstream news. This major shift allows us to peek behind the wizard's curtain and ask whether technological mediums control culture or if cultural ideas shape technology. The two seem linked in a struggle for dominance.

Great ideas definitely have a place in shaping the course of history. Is it fair to say that until artificial intelligence is developed, though, technology does not exist without the imagination and resourcefulness of humans? After all, it was Steve Jobs' creative ideas and passion for quality music, matched with the technological genius of Tony Fadell that led to the revolutionary development of the iPod. The idea behind the technology pushed the innovation. Then, and only then, did the small technology box shape culture and make music ubiquitous while at the same time create communication barriers. Earphones are essentially earplugs which shun people and effectively communicate, "Don't bother me." This is what McLuhan was talking about; technology sends a message, yet still only a ripple made by a pebble.

Great economic ideas, from Adam Smith's capitalism to Karl Marx's communism, are like massive boulders that were pushed over a cliff into the bay, which caused a series of giant waves to crash on continental shores. Every society on the planet has been affected by these two ideas. Needless to say, it is obvious that ideas drive change and possess the power to shape culture.

Going back to Jared Diamond's subject matter in *Guns, Germs and Steel*- Are there greater forces of change beyond ideas and technology? Does evolution determine our destiny? Jared Diamond points out that the Native Americans died because they had not been previously exposed to the animals that carried the diseases against which the Europeans had developed immunity over time. The Europeans had experienced more contact with the infected domestic beasts and gradually overcame their threat. Therefore, some conclude that evolution is in control, yet indifferent to the survival of the human race. It seems we must mutate or die.

Diamond considers another factor in the evolution process, geography. The deadly diseases originated in animals that lived at around the same latitude. Since Europe runs mostly East-to-West and North America spans a greater distance North-to-South, the Europeans had a denser cohabitation with its domestic animals. If the variables in evolution had been different, we all might be worshipping the Aztec god Quetzalcoatl. How arbitrary is that?

If fate is at work through mutation, and our destiny is determined by where and when we are born, perhaps leaders should leave well enough alone and let evolution initiate change. Diamond disagrees: "Without human inventiveness all of us would still be cutting our meat with stone tools and eating it raw like our ancestors of a million years ago." What little control we possess still amounts to tremendous power to change our world. Ideas and technology still play an important role in shaping our futures.

Types of Change

Sociologists disagree about which change driver is most powerful to shape culture but three make the short list of most experts- ideas, technology, and power. I conflate class struggle, factions, political elitism, and military might into one category of power. In suit with systems thinking, though, it's never just one thing. Most change occurs from a combination of driving forces. Leaders must harness many different forces to catalyze change and still recognize that forces outside their control are working against them and others to their advantage. Peter Bishop, a futurist and professor of future studies at the University of Clear Lake in Houston, Texas, considers not only the driving forces of change but also the different types of change.

According to Bishop's theory, Events, Cycles, Trends, and Wildcards are observable changes that impact society. Examples of such events could be the passing of new legislation or the succession of a new leader. Seasons are cyclical as are markets, products, and businesses. Trends are qualified by the word "more" or "less." For ox ample, if over a measurable timeframe the number of people eating organic food increases, or is more than the last reported number, this could be considered a trend (if it holds long enough). Wildcards are un-expected events, like the fall of the Berlin Wall.

Bishop explains that we experience change as a punctuated equilibrium. "Taken from the theory of biological evolution, punctuated equilibrium consists of eras, relatively long periods of stability and con-tinuous change separated by shorter periods of instability and disruptive change." So, change is either incremental, like beach erosion or it is transformational, like a hurricane that destroys a levy.

Thomas Kuhn, who coined the term "paradigm shift," is most famous for explaining transformational change. Paradigms are ac-cepted norms that are broken when an anomaly appears. As the Ses-ame Street song goes, "One of these things doesn't belong." In re-sponse, scientists experiment until they discover a new paradigm that explains the weird phenomenon. This is what Kuhn called scientific revolution. One of the main questions remaining is whether new para-digms are completely new or if they transcend _and_ include the old paradigm. (What will scientists do if Einstein's theory of relativity is de-bunked by the discovery of neutrinos which supposedly travel faster than the speed of light? It is not likely that Einstein will be so easily dis-regarded.) Most people realize the danger in throwing the baby out with the bath water so they are not hasty to adopt new ideas or shift their paradigm too quickly.

Sometimes, fine lines are drawn. Evolutionists discredit creationism, forcing a split between science and religion. One is based on fact, so it is said, and the other on faith, which leads people to believe that the two are incompatible. Ultimately, though, we return to a simple truth- humans feel a need to interpret change and explain their reality. They refuse to let weird stuff happen without inventing reasons for it or deriving meaning from it. We tell stories to put the pieces together so everything makes sense.

Interpreting & Instigating Change

Comically, in the attempt to make sense of things is where things tend to fall apart. Philosophers prefer reason and logic to comprehend life. They have beat around the bush, set the bush on fire, and planted new bushes in an effort to define reality, speak truth, and learn what is good. Scientists prefer empiricism, what can be observed and measured. They claim objectivity and argue that reality is what we can test, prove, and reproduce. Postmodernists prefer experience to make sense of the world. They believe in relativity which validates everyone's point of view. And religious people prefer authoritative sources like the Bible, Qur'an, or a cult leader to explain human existence and purpose. Herein lies the foundation of knowledge: *reason*, *empiricism*, *experience*, and *authority*- the four pillars of knowledge. We know what we know because we accept the information in one or more of these forms. But is there another way to know something?

Hope is a way of knowing that bends the rules, in a manner of speaking. In the 1800's William Pitt and William Wilberforce conspired against the British Parliament to bring an end to the slave trade. In the movie *Amazing Grace* Pitt says, "We'll do it because we are too naive to know that it's impossible." The only knowledge for success they had to go on was their conviction that slavery was evil and that it must cease. Hope sometimes goes against reason, even against the empirical data because it envisions a compelling alternative reality.

There are two ways to arrive at this preferred future that must be considered. The idea of "Progress" suggests that we can get there from here, wherever "there" may be because of the boundless human spirit which has repeatedly triumphed over seemingly impossible odds. The assumption is that if we keep doing more of what we have been doing, we will arrive at our destination. Hope sometimes works like that but occasionally it requires what Ted Peters calls "adventus." Adventus is understood in this way- "Hope sees the world as holding possibilities that are not merely extensions of past trends or a continuation of the present state of affairs. To 'hope against hope' is to recognize that the new which I desire is not merely the expected outcome of present trends." In other words, hope requires us to believe that only emergent realities, the result of a unique combination of circumstances, can take us where we want to go.

It is like in the movie *Back to the Future* where Marty (played by Michael J. Fox) tries to talk to "Doc" (played by Christopher Lloyd) about his time travel arrangements. Marty reminds the Doctor that they do not have enough road in his neighborhood to get the time machine (a Delorean car) up to 88mph, the necessary speed to activate the flux capacitor which would allow them to travel into the future. The "Doc" puts a banana peel in the gas tank and says, "Where we're going, we don't need roads." The car hovers, zips into the sky, and they transport back into the future. Something in the future allows us to do what we cannot do right now.

The future is a mystery in the present and people usually choose one or more anchors of hope to make sure the mystery does not become a horror story. Christians believe that God is acting on their behalf and the future is primarily in His control. Others in society hope politicians are acting for the common good and that they will shape the future responsibly. Business, on the other hand, is about competition and the fierce environment makes it hard to believe that anyone is working on behalf of anyone else. Business also has the difficulty of "pleasing all the people all the time."

Stakeholders, customers and employees must be considered. Who's looking out for whom? How does everyone involved in an organization in one way or another arrive at this wonderful alternative future reality leaders like to call their "vision"? The two closest things to *adventus* hope in a business context are partnership and innovation, which allow organizations to accomplish what it cannot do presently on its own.

Strategic Foresight & Habits of Hope

In a business context hope is a difficult sell. You're not going to walk into your boss' office and say, "I've got this great strategy to initiate change around here. It's called 'hang your hat on hope." Executives want analytics, predictable forecasts, and market trend data. Get real. As one de-motivator plaque says, "You're not getting paid to believe in the power of your dreams." I therefore recommend you take a different approach. There are distinct ways to look at the future in what Bishop calls the "cone of plausibility" that are consistent with a hope paradigm and relevant to the business world.

Within the cone are three futures- the *possible*, the *plausible*, and the *proferable*. Most likely your organization initiates change with the preferable future in mind and with prepared contingency plans if the unpleasant "plausible" happens. Many companies now investigate the "possible" future via scenario planning, made popular by Peter Swartz and Royal Dutch/Shell Oil Company in the 1970's. Depending on an organization's maturity, all three perspectives are considered in the strategic planning process.

Hope deals in all three types of futures. Hope practices scenario development-*story telling, where* promises and threats are identified and where numerical data is fleshed out. Hope relies on forecasting the "plausible" to provide a *constant*- something that gives reality a future identity and upon which some action can be justified. And Hope envisions an attractive alternative reality, a preferred future that serves to motivate people to venture forward into the unknown. Entrepreneurs survive on this kind of energy. If they didn't believe their product or service was superior to what was currently available, there would be no reason to risk any investment.

Hope is involved in every type of observable change- events, cycles, trends, and wildcards. Hope is the reason for every human-initiated transformational change. There would be no class struggle if the poor did not fight for equality, if they did not desire a different reality. Cures for sickness would not be found if people did not hope to end needless suffering. iPhones and XBOXes would not exist if people

65

didn't long for communication, competition, fun, and diversion. Of course "bad" change happens when we don't get what we hoped for. Even so, someone probably walked away happy from that change.

It's not that change cannot happen without our practice of hope. Change happens period, but without hope, we cannot harness it, or understand its meaning. Abraham Lincoln said that indecision is really a choice to let someone else decide the future. In other words, failing to plan is a planning to fail. Strategic planning means developing habits of hope to actively shape the future.

As a leader, you must involve your team, your organization, and your customers or clients in this process. People need a good "why" when they are encouraged to leave what is comfortable in exchange for sacrifice and hard work. Getting people to buy a new and improved product demands a good "why" too. We cannot do business with an evolution driven approach which only answers the question "how." How a team functions, how a product works, how a new medicine prevents infection leaves people asking "why." Leaders must be dealers in hope because hope provides the "why" to change. "How" leads to despair because it only offers explanation, whereas hope answers "why" and offers understanding and inspiration.

There are two ways to arrive at the "why" of the matter- through pain or gain. Leaders who initiate the change they hope for, but exclude the hopes of others, only create frustration and hopelessness. Force and fear are the best methods to control people in this type of change management. Threatening to fire someone, to reduce their salary, or give a poor review can snap an employee into submission and ensure their cooperation. Dictators favor this negative approach to change management because force and fear usually produce quicker results.

Dr. Larry Stout points out, though, that people only respond to these measures to a limited degree. As the threat diminishes people resume their former behavior. Conversely, people who pursue gain will go beyond expectations to achieve their goals.

Psychologist C.R. Snyder explains this emergent quality, the ever-expanding growth of hope. Particular hopes act not only as the ends people desire but as the means to further ends. Once someone possesses what they hope for, that possession serves as a means to another greater end. As the theologian Jürgen Moltmann describes, hope can be understood as an expanding spiral. The capacity for what people hope for increases as they see their hopes materialize. This is how hope matures.

Everyone is born with the instinct to hope but it remains immature if it is not properly nurtured. Some people do not experience hope as an expanding spiral, but as a cycle of increasing disappointment. You have probably heard many parents tell their kids, "Don't get your hopes up." They tried hope once and got burned, so they decided it was better to not hope for anything big. Lowering expectations is a failure to understand the powerful emergent behavior of hope.

To explain how hope matures, the contemporary philosopher Dr Patrick Shade makes the distinction between hopes, hopefulness, and habits of hope. In *Habits of Hope*, Shade points out that hopes "have some specific end, whether object or an activity, which we seek to realize." One could associate this with Stephen Covey's second habit of highly effective people, "Begin with the end in mind."

Shade clarifies **hopefulness** as the open-mindedness of hoping. He says, "... it is an orientation to open, attentive readiness to possibilities that promise satisfaction." Believing that God is the source of satisfaction, theologian Walter Brueggemann would insist that in order for hope to thrive in our hearts, "God must be free to work a surprise." Shade would qualify this as hopefulness.

"Habits of hope" are developed as competencies, or skills, to achieve goals. "Chief among them are persistence, general resourcefulness, and courage," suggests Shade. Practicing hope and developing it as a habit requires an emotional maturation process that balances a fixed focus while remaining flexible.

I agree that a leader must possess certain competencies to develop his or her habit of hope. I believe Dr. Larry Stout's leadership model found in his book, *Time for a Change,* offers the most succinct understanding of leadership and successfully identifies the universal competencies all good leaders possess. Not surprisingly, his model is consistent with my hope paradigm, as are the other hope frameworks I have mentioned.

Shade's idea of hopefulness exists throughout the hope diamond I explained in chapter three, which emphasizes that hope is an open system. One can hope to graduate in four years and still be open to a different future, perhaps one where they meet a girl, fall in love, take a six month tour of Europe together, and then come back to their studies.

Immature hope is closed to the future and *not* open to the possibility that things will work out better than planned, that a new plan may emerge, or that better means and ends may be revealed. Immature hope hogs the glory for a team achievement. Immature hope is success without significance. Hope breaks down in a closed system.

Shade's hopefulness is very pragmatic in that it makes us more "productive and more creative people." But hope is even more effective than that as an agent of change. For example, try to lose weight or struggle through another day in a difficult marriage without hope. Hope "sustains and energizes us," explains Shade, and offers meaning to piece our world together.

Without this meaning-making tool, life resorts to putting a 5000 piece puzzle together without the cover picture on the box to go by. This might seem counterintuitive but observe individuals or organizations where success outpaces the ability for people to make sense of the growth, you will see the warning signs of hopelessness.

Two acquaintances of mine are both wildly successful, yet they are prone to despair because their identity has not caught up with the multiplicative power of success. Their achievements surpassed their vision and now they do not know what to hope for. It's the Rock Star phenomenon- Become rich, get everything you thought you wanted, party hard, start using drugs, gamble, and flush your life down the toilet. Sports figures and lottery winners are known to do the same thing. It's not a boredom problem, it's an identity issue, a trip into a world that doesn't make sense.

Robert W. Terry, author of *Authentic Leadership,* spells out that true leaders understand reality and help others make sense of it. They work to figure out what is going on, but then, rather than tell everyone all the answers, the leader empowers others to make the discovery for themselves.

Understanding reality is important but imagining an alternative reality is absolutely essential to shaping culture as a dealer in hope. Tom Costello, NBC News Correspondent echoes this point- "Ivan Illich was once asked what is the most revolutionary way to change society. Is it violent revolution or gradual reform? He gave a careful answer.

Neither. If you want to change society, then you must tell an alternative story."

A Look at Culture

Reality in Africa is harsh. There is a tree in Africa that speaks of the life there and reminds us that things are not as they could and should be. The legend has it that God came up to this tree and it had no fruit for him. So God ripped it out of the earth and put it back upside-down. That is why the branches look like roots that reach to the sky. In Senegal, a Western coastal country in Africa, life seems fruitless and upside-down. The children, who should be the hope of any nation's future, are made to suffer the most. Tens of thousands beg in the streets for food to survive. Worse yet, they beg to earn money for their teachers. They are called the Talibe, disciples of Islamic religious leaders.

Talibe boys are not called by their name. They only have one single common identity- their name is Talibe. Around the age of six, boys are recruited by a teacher, the Marabou, to live with him and learn from him. The Marabou promises the parents that he will provide shelter, food, clothing, and a topnotch education primarily focused on learning the Qur'an. Many parents are too poor to care for their many children so this alternative seems attractive. Others fear falling out of favor with such a powerful religious figure.

In Senegalese society the Marabou are heroes. People wear charms around their necks with pictures of their favorite Marabou and taxi drivers put portraits of popular Marabou on the dashboards of their cabs or dangle them from their rearview mirrors. It is believed that a Marabou can protect your life. Even Politicians seek their blessing. But this is Senegal, where life is upside-down, where the nation's heroes are also enslaving the children.

Senegal's history is dark. The slave trade devastated this country for over four hundred years and still today human life is devalued. Because the economic situation is dire, the Marabou force their disciples to beg in the streets to pay his salary. The promises made to the parents go unfulfilled mostly, except for the Islamic education. The children have to fend for themselves. They sleep on the ground or concrete floors of homes under construction. When they are not in class Talibe beg door to door for food scraps. Talibe has no place to bathe and because of this unsanitary way of life, most boys become hosts to parasites.

Defining Culture

Surprisingly, many Talibe hope to become a Marabou. This is culture. Though it might seem backwards, upside-down, unjust, corrupt, or just plain wrong, it is the accepted culture of the people living in Senegal.

Culture has been difficult to define over the last hundred-plus years, as anthropologists admit. In 1871, Edward Tylor wrote *Primitive Culture* and defined culture as "that complex whole which includes knowledge, belief, art, law, morals, custom, and any other capacities and habits acquired by man as a member of society." Simply put for this audience, culture is the way an organization conducts business.The theologian Kevin Vanhoozer takes a shot at categorizing the parts that make up this whole by describing the behavior of culture. "In particular, culture does four things: culture *communicates*, culture *orients*, culture *reproduces*, and culture *cultivates*."

Communication

Every culture has a language, the signs and symbols that provide understanding through shared interpretation. In business, marketing is the main voice of communication between the producer and consumer. As Vanhoozer says, perfume is more than a chemical composition that produces an enjoyable scent. Companies market this product to create a broader, more interesting meaning. "For instance, some perfumes are named after abstract, almost mystical notions like *Truth* or *Eternity*. Others have names that connote murkier moral ground: *Obsession*, *Decadence*, *Babylon*."   But culture does not automatically accept every message that is communicated.

Orientation

Culture also orients people to bring order to information. "While cultural works and worlds of meaning do have a cognitive dimension, affecting what we think, they also have affective and evaluative dimensions influencing our likes and dislikes as well as our sense of right and wrong," Vanhoozer explains. So, the message marketing sends is forced to echo what culture approves, most of the time. Perhaps that is why in a progressively tolerant society like the U.S., the seven deadly sins are now the seven marketing imperatives. However, shaping culture does require a new message or an old one communicated in a new way, not just saying what everyone already knows. Similar to what the priest Henri Nouwen says about why we like books and music, marketing must "express what culture vaguely feels" if it is to persuade.

Reproduction

"Culture spreads beliefs, values, ideas, fashions, and practices from one social group to another," Vanhoozer observes. The documentary, *Merchants of Cool*, put out by Frontline, reveals why companies invest so many resources to understand the youth culture. Marketing moguls acknowledge the reproductive power of culture to either approve a product/ service or squash it. I suggest that teenagers are perhaps the least fragmented subculture within society, allowing messages to flow contiguously. If harnessed, companies can generate great profits or, if untapped, will be run out of business by the competition. However, the accessibility of diverse options via the internet works to fragment culture, the reason niche marketing is strategic. The new challenge to sell product is to find niches that are contiguous to each other and where the boundaries are permeable so that marketing dollars (messages) can reach more people.

Cultivation

Reproduction alone can be considered a shallow function of culture. Just because people copy each other does not mean that ideas or beliefs take root and stick. Cultivation creates the environment where ideas can be sown, where values take root. In business, the result would be the difference between compliance versus commitment. In culture, it's the difference between fads and values. Cultivation means passing on values to the next generation. Creating a hopescape is the cultivation process of sowing values into new images of the future.

Shaping Senegal

France has put tremendous pressure on Senegal because children being forced to beg to pay a teacher's salary is repulsive to Western culture. However, natives of Senegal resent the French influence, especially the era of colonization which included years of the slave trade. Cultivating a new worldview or planting a new idea in the mind of the Senegalese people will not take root if sown by the French. The reason for this is that the ground of culture was exploited, not cultivated by leadership.

Some ideas will not grow in certain cultures under the present conditions just as quality coffee will not grow outside a 1,800 to 3,600 ft. altitude. First, the conditions must change. A hopescape must be created, an oasis discovered in Senegal's expanding desert.

Shaping Culture

There is another tree in Africa that grows in the patio of a foreigner living in Senegal. Gilberth is from Costa Rica and he moved to Ties, Senegal with his wife Damaris and two grown children. They are cultivating and shaping culture. Talibe boys are received daily for a simple breakfast and provided a place to shower in the evening. Periodically the boys are given a fresh set of clothes and a full course meal.

Gilberth and Damaris come from difficult economic circumstances of their own but they create abundance out of very little. Damaris teaches the adult women to sew, cook, make and sell crafts in the market and she teaches them how to read and write. Instead of retiring to the beaches of their home country, this couple decided to start all over again and foster 10 Senegalese children, some of whom would have otherwise been handed over to a Marabou and left to fend for themselves.

Initially this work brought negative attention from neighbors and the police requested that government officials investigate. When they discovered the purpose of the project and observed how the children were treated, the government granted Gilberth and Damaris complete freedom and authority to continue their work. Being that they are not Muslims, it was surprising that the government validated this couple's influence in the community. Gilberth and Damaris have been invited to cultivate in this place and their love, humility, and acts of service are digging up the ground. They offer an alternative reality and people are receptive to this new way of life.

Consider their approach. Gilberth and Damaris identify with the people. They live among them, not set apart. They try to speak their language and understand the Senegalese culture. It is not the rich giving handouts to the poor. It is the poor teaching the poor not just how to survive, but how to thrive in the community. This is the I-Thou solidarity of hopeful relationships. The Costa Ricans have linked their destiny with the people of Senegal. Gilberth has even befriended the Marabou, not usurped their authority or openly condemned their behavior. Gilberth and Damaris inspire hope to the people living on the edge of the expanding Sahara Desert. Their lives and work create an oasis, not a mirage in this place.

Dealers in hope cultivate to lead change and ultimately shape culture. To understand this better, we will consider these four dealers in hope: Barack Obama, Steve Jobs, Mike Morhaime, and Moses. Initially successful in leading change, Moses eventually failed because he could never break the slave mentality of his generation. Mike Morhaime

CEO of Blizzard and creator of the online game World of Warcraft, succeeded in cultivating an entire virtual world. Steve Jobs, along with his team at Apple, created the Cult of Mac and they are clearly trendsetters in their industry. Barack Obama managed to become an icon during the presidential race, creating "brand Obama," and became the first black president of the United States. These leaders inspire us and we can stand in awe of their achievements. But we should recognize hope as the phenomenon behind the scenes, the condition necessary for legendary leadership exploits.

Barack Obama

age 40+

Dealer in hope

Leading Change & Shaping culture:

First Black President of the United States.

Even if you voted for Hillary or McCain or you abstained from casting your ballot, Obama still has a lot to teach us about the hope phenomenon. You are probably wondering who I voted for so you can better discern whether any bias might skew my objectivity. Well, I did vote for Obama. Yet, I am still undecided whether Obama is a catalyst for true hope or whether it is all political mirage. I do consider the time up until his election a true wave of hope and enough of an instance in shaping culture to warrant a chapter in this book. As President, however, Obama might become too much of a pragmatist to be truly dealing with authentic hope. We will have to see.

As a diligent student of hope it was somewhat natural to identify the words and actions that catalyzed hope during the elections. I willing jumped on that train to see where it was going and I cast my vote for Obama because he is an agent of change. I was tired of 16 years of the same old game of politics. Unfortunately, I cannot explain further my reasoning for doing so because I don't want tangent emotions to take us in a different direction than what I believe true hope has in store for us. Our theme is hope more than it is Obama. To simplify things I mainly consider the shaping and leading that he did previous to Election Day. This is a case study of sorts in reflection of that time period.

Authentic Leadership

"Yes we can!" Obama proclaimed. The YouTube video compiling a montage of celebrities singing these words created a soundtrack for not only this speech but for his entire campaign. This message has been viewed more than eighteen million times online. Surprisingly, a lot of excitement surrounded Obama, who appeared to only barely win the democratic nomination. The Presidential election cannot be considered a landslide victory either. However, not since Lyndon B. Johnson has a President enjoyed 54% of the popular vote. Obama is the third most popular democratic candidate in the last 150 years.

Even though electoral votes, not popularity, count towards winning the election, the popular vote can grant immanent power to a President to make changes almost without asking permission, like a blank check. President Bush announced that he intended to fulfill his inherent mandate from the people, having received 52% of the popular vote in 2004. In light of Bush's ratings during his final days, which were under 30%, Obama chose not to assume or proclaim any mandate.

Almost antithetical to Bush, Obama rained on his own parade. Perhaps fearful of the "hype" generated from crossing such a monumental threshold as becoming the first black President, Obama pitched a reality check in his inaugural address. "For everywhere we look, there is work to be done," he challenged. He threw off the mantle of savior and threw the responsibility book on the people. Obama also reminded Americans, "On this day, we gather because we have chosen hope over fear, unity of purpose over conflict and discord."

As in the days of John F. Kennedy, it is not, "Ask of Obama what he can do for the country." Rather, the pivotal word is "we," "We" is in the middle of the phrase, "Yes we can!" As I wrote earlier, "we" makes hope possible, not individualism. Astutely, Obama realized that hope is not wielded by one man or one woman and he relinquished a personal mandate in order to empower the people.

This verbal action, to relinquish power, is a paradigm shift in leadership. Gone are the days when Americans will tolerate charismatic leadership. Too many prominent figures, like televangelists and corporate con-artists, have risen and raised public emotions only to shame and disappoint followers with their catastrophic failures. I history records even worse icons of charisma, leaders like Hitler and Stalin who revealed themselves as fascists. Charisma deals in hype and is quite contagious, like hope, but instead of love and faith to accompany it, hype produces fear and doubt. What followers want now is authentic leadership. In the *Leadership Challenge*, Kouzes and Posner's research revealed that trust is the number one characteristic followers want in a leader. Authenticity inspires trust.

Authentic means real and true. No politician could spin a *hope* slogan or a *change* slogan in these times without authenticity. "I love you" is an absurd expression coming from a prostitute. Likewise, politicians are banned from using the word hope because they always break their promises. So, how did Obama get away with it? Was it a Walt Disney Mickey Mouse trick- take what everyone is afraid of and make it cute and funny? Did Obama slap a *hope* sticker on the elephant in the room and hypnotize us with unbelievable promises like "I will not take any money from lobbyists." In regard to normal jockeying with these wielders of money and power, Obama said, "We're not going to play that game."

Robert Terry's book, *Authentic Leadership: Courage in Action*, pinpoints how authenticity is distinctive: "Power wielders are to be distinguished from leaders. Power wielders seek to accomplish their own will, whether or not it is the will of others. Leaders seek to meet the will of both leaders and followers. 'To control things- tools, mineral resources, money, energy- is an act of power, not leadership, for things have no motives. Power wielders may treat people as things. Leaders may not. All leaders are actual or potential power holders, but not all power holders are leaders'." In other words, authentic leaders have higher regard for people than for power.

President Bush's attitude towards polling unfortunately communicated that he didn't care what the people thought. He stuck to his guns, literally, and lost the trust of more than 70% of Americans. President Clinton, on the other hand, perhaps polled too often, possibly an insecurity stemming from the public's lack of confidence in his moral behavior.

Authentic leaders listen to others but they are still the leader, the one who harnesses and directs the energy and power of resources. Barack Obama, obviously possessing some charisma, is more strikingly authentic. Obama does not allow himself to get carried away or express anger often like most charismatic speakers. Hope is the difference. There is no need to instill fear or create euphoria to control the masses when hope is at the heart of the message.

Obama seems to be authentic as Terry describes it. "If leadership is to discern what is true and real, what is actual and what is virtual, then leadership must be open to others' interpretations of events. Leadership, therefore, is inherently dialogical. It encourages the bumping of one perspective with another. It reaches for shared meaning among diverse meanings, shared value among conflicting values. It seeks to reveal what is happening and what ought to happen," suggests Terry. Obama's transparency and deliberation in answering questions shows that he is listening to the questions more than avoiding them. He might not appreciate the steering some agendas have in their questioning, but Obama works at dialogue.

In the presidential debate with Rick Warren, Obama was asked, "OK, we've got one last question — I've got a bunch more, but let me ask you one about evil. Does evil exist? And if it does, do we ignore it? Do we negotiate with it? Do we contain it? Do we defeat it?" After acknowledging that evil does exist Obama added, "Now, the one thing that I think is very important is for us to have some humility in how we approach the issue of confronting evil, because a lot of evil's been perpetrated based on the claim that we were trying to confront evil." This statement reveals quite a lot juxtaposed McCain's answer to the same question. With no hesitation whatsoever McCain responded, "Defeat it.

A couple of points. One, if I'm president of the United States, my friends, if I have to follow him to the gates of hell, I will get bin Laden and bring him to justice. I will do that. And I know how to do that. I will get that done. (APPLAUSE). No one, no one should be allowed to take thousands of American — innocent American lives."

McCain's answer lacked the humility Obama was talking about. There is no doubt that McCain is a war hero and understands leadership, even calling it "stewardship," a philosophy that reflects concern for people over power. Yet his words reflect the individualism that snuffs out hope. Obama identified with the millions throughout history who were oppressed and killed by those who claimed the moral high ground. He even confessed being guilty of the same by using the word "we" over and over again. McCain's response highlighted individualism. "I will get bin Laden." "I will do that." "I know how to do that."

Humility is one characteristic of authenticity. It is a form of honesty. Yes, we are all guilty of doing evil in the name of good. It's called selfishness, which sometimes masquerades as righteousness. Authenticity is transparent and reflects what is real and true. Ideologies sometimes justify evil actions and call them good, skewing what is real and true. Ideologies are based on "us" versus "them" and the word "we" never means to include.

Along with the idea of shared vision and shared meaning, Obama understands better than most that America is a pluralistic society and therefore he rejects ideology. He is too pragmatic for that. Without this authenticity to attest to America's mistakes, to America's harmful ideologies, the hope and change slogans would have fallen flat on their faces. Being black is to understand that ideology even trumps the Constitution of the United States. It is now over one hundred years later since the 13th and 14th amendment were passed that blacks can finally say that America is a land of equal opportunity, from the top-down. Yet, Obama never played the race card or made his candidacy a "black thing." It was always "We the People." This authentic approach to the world opened people's hearts to hope, to the possibility that hope and politics might be compatible. Can the two co-exist? "Yes they can."

"Sticky" Messages

Authentic hope is a message that sticks, that people remember and internalize. Malcolm Gladwell, author of The Tipping Point, suggests that in order for a movement to erupt, there must be a "sticky" message. Can words start movements? Maybe you remember these phrases- "Change we can believe in." "Nothing can stand in the way of millions of voices calling for change." "We are the change we've been looking for."

One expert said that any democrat could have won the 2008 election because what the people wanted was change, anything different from "more of the same." I disagree. America was not saying, "Any ol' change will do." People had specific things in mind, a mental picture of what change looked like and Obama expressed that. McCain knew this too. He ran with the same slogan and even called himself the "Maverick." But it didn't stick. No matter how hard McCain tried to shake the comparison with Bush, he could not separate himself from his predecessor in the eyes of the public. Obviously a "sticky" message has to be more than just words.

"There has never been anything false about hope," Obama said. The word false stands out in his cadence and repetition in the

YouTube speech. What made Obama's message stick is that it did not seem false. Hope, as a slogan, is trite and unbelievable in this epoch of American culture. People do not trust politicians. They are scandalous. Even with such great popularity during the primaries, Hillary Clinton could not escape her checkered past and her association with a cunning husband who was almost impeached while President. Obama, on the other hand, had no real political history and few sketchy ties.

Everyone knows from reading the disclaimers on movies and TV shows that the views expressed by the actors do not necessarily represent the organization that produced the film. Though associated with Reverend Wright and William Avery, racist and radical, Obama succeeded in distancing himself from them when the moment called for it. At the same time he closed the gap between himself and those who fought for equal rights in an admirable fashion.

Barack Obama's speech on race highlights his fervent hope in the American "experiment." Talking about one of the tasks set by his administration, Obama said that they must "continue the long march of those who came before us." With "common hopes" Americans could continue to perfect the Union. It is one thing for a white candidate to echo the words of the Constitution, words that have stuck in the minds of millions for over two hundred years. It is quite another thing for a black man to express his undying belief in the idea of a "more perfect Union" when "America's original sin of slavery," as Obama put it, had oppressed his race for so long.

Obama's message sticks not simply because of his eloquent speech but because of who he is, a black man convinced that America's history is deeply connected to the more perfect future of a united and equal people. By appealing to the "better angels of our nature"

Obama found an America that was ready for its first black leader, the President of the United States.

Imagine

"Scrub language of all religious content and we forfeit the imagery and terminology through which millions of Americans understand both their personal morality and social justice. Imagine Lincoln's Second Inaugural Address without reference to 'the judgments of the Lord,' or King's 'I Have a Dream' speech without reference to 'all of God's children.' Their summoning of a higher truth helped inspire what had seemed impossible and move the nation to embrace a common destiny." -Barack Obama, *Audacity of Hope*

Did Obama echo the voice of the people and together, with their hopes, empower the people to imagine an alternative reality, a different future?

> *Review*: There is a process for how hope develops.

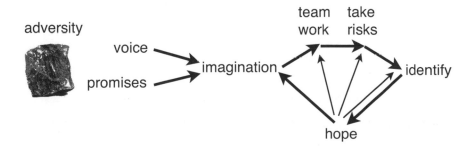

Remember, only in a high pressure environment can coal turn into a diamond, so particular conditions are necessary to catalyze hope. Once the hopescape is set, adversity can be turned into hope. The bottom-line is that all four elements in the diamond must exist for authentic hope to exist. Imagination without action is just wishful thinking.

Adversity

Alan I. Abramowitz, a political expert wrote, "At the beginning of the fall campaign the mood of the American public was already extremely sour. Real incomes had been falling and home foreclosures and unemployment had been rising for months." Then all hell broke loose as one major company after another declared bankruptcy or financial instability. The Economic Crisis of 2008 hit hard and experts summarized the damage as worse than anything since the Great Depression. On top of this, America was fighting two wars. Map the Fallen and Google Earth record that by October 1, 2008, there had been 5,466 U.S. military casualties. Iran and North Korea were hostile and making threats, and Darfur was still a genocide unchecked.

Voice

Most political experts agree that there were three main important issues that concerned the public: the slowing economy, the war in Iraq, and the end of the Bush era. President Bush did not even attend the Republican National Convention as the McCain administration and the Republican Party worked to distance itself from the unpopular incumbent. Eighty percent of Americans believed the country was on the wrong track and they voiced it in the polls. People wanted change and their hope took form as Obama's promises mixed with the people's voiced frustrations.

In *The Year of Obama: How Barack Obama Won the White House*, Larry Sabato illuminates many driving forces that affected the outcome of the primaries and the election. "Some may be surprised that Obama was able to secure 20 percent of the vote among conservatives; surely this was a 'time for change' phenomenon," Sabato wrote. The environment was set for change, but the "change" had to echo the people's interests and values.

America was, and still is, experiencing a culture shift as climate change and the pressure of globalization force society to adapt to new conditions. New emerging values like sustainability, global partnerships, fuel independence, and pursuit of green technology are now high priority. The promises made by each candidate revealed whether or not they "got it." How each imagined and painted the future affected how people voted. At the age of 72, McCain struggled to convince Americans he embraced the new way of thinking this new environment demanded. His words did not express what the people vaguely felt and his actions showed that he thought like a Senator, not like a President. (McCain suspended his campaign to help pass an economic stimulus bill. This was interpreted as Senator's work and unbecoming of a future president.)

As Congress' popularity reached record lows, Obama's lack of experience actually worked in his favor. This fact is incomprehensible to the older generations who believe expertise and experience should determine who runs the country. Expertise defined as knowledge of how

Washington works, though, is a double-edge sword. The majority of the public wanted someone who thought like them, not a typical politician. Hiillary and McCain both knew first hand the ins and outs of the game but Obama was creating a new game.

Promises

PolitiFact.com created the Obameter to track the President's progress on over 500 promises he made while running for office. Status is rated as such as of April 2009:

No Action	397
In the Works	64
Stalled	9
Promise Kept	30
Compromise	8
Promise Broken	6

At this rate, Obama fulfills about 3 promises every ten to fifteen days. If the trend continues Obama will fulfill approximately 340 promises or 68% of all 514 by the end of his first term. By anyone's standards that would be considered a miraculous success in politics.

As I said earlier, hope cannot exist without a promise. Obama has made his fair share. This to-do list is daunting and perhaps only feasible because Democrats enjoy a filibuster proof majority, which has not existed since 1937 when Franklin D. Roosevelt held office and be cause the promises echo what the majority of American citizens voiced. The focus of this book, however, is on how Obama shaped culture and led change *before* he became President. Hope will quickly fade if he breaks his major promises but that analysis is for another book.

Obama made three essential promises to America during his campaign that emancipated the public's imagination:

1. The Economy & Environment- Obama will create 2.5 million jobs by 2011 and 5 million "green" jobs within 10 years to get America back to work.
2. Foreign Policy- Obama will order responsible withdraw from Iraq on the first day of office and work to build a new relationship with Muslim countries and with the world based on mutual respect.
3. Healthcare- Obama will propose a plan to ensure choice, reduce costs and cover the 50 million Americans currently without healthcare insurance.

Big whoop, you might think. Every politician makes promises. Notice, though, how specific Obama's promises are. Obama used numbers to trump any vague promises his opponents would make and he set himself up for accountability, which was sorely lacking in the days leading up to his campaign. A failure in leadership set Obama up for his biggest promise:

"Make no mistake: We need to end an era in Washington where accountability has been absent, oversight has been overlooked, your tax dollars have been turned over to wealthy CEOs and the well-connected corporations. You need leadership you can trust to work for you, not for the special interests who have had their thumb on the scale.

And together, we will tell Washington, and their lobbyists, that their days of setting the agenda are over. They have not funded my campaign. You have. They will not run my White House. You'll help me run my White House."

This promise greatly distinguished Obama from his opponents. It was not going to be business as usual. The implicit promise was, "I'm setting up a new system where the old rules to the old game won't work anymore because they only benefit those already in power." Obama's promise of transparency and accountability took Washington and Wall Street by surprise and it resonated with the public fed up with poor leadership.

If I were tracking Obama's promises and level of hope, I would have to point out that Politifact.com rates the promise to keep lobbyists from interfering with politics as a broken promise. The promise was kept during Obama's campaign as he even returned money donated by lob-byists. However, when he selected William Lynn, former Raytheon lob-byist, as Deputy Defense Secretary, it was concluded that Obama broke his promise. Raytheon is ranked number six in the world as a defense contractor. Conflict of interest? Maybe. The Obama admini-stration, which highly values transparency, has been quite elusive re-garding the lobbyist issue since 2009. I point this out only so my read-ers realize that I am not blinded by hope.

Leaders do break their promises from time to time. Sometimes they must compromise and that too seems like they're not keeping their word. The important thing is not to put too much stock in promises.

They can be exciting but just as powerfully disappointing. Hope cannot exist without a promise but neither is hope forged by pretty words and flattery. Obama did not simply blow smoke, however. He implemented the hope paradigm that eventually shaped the American culture.

Team Work

On November 4, 2008, Obama had 2,397,253 friends on Facebook. McCain had 622,860. There were over 100,000 videos about Obama viewed 889 million times, whereas McCain only had 64,092 videos with 554 million viewings. "By the end of the campaign cycle, one million people had signed up for Obama's text-messaging program. The e-mail databank had entries for more than 13 million people, who had received over 1 billion messages from the campaign, with more than 7,000 different messages. On MyBarackObama.com, supporters created 2 million profiles, planned 200,000 offline events, posted 400,000 blog entries, and started more than 35,000 volunteer groups. Approximately 3 million calls were made in the final four days of the campaign using MyBO's virtual phone-banking platform." (Sabato)

Obama's campaign was a grass roots movement. Millions were mobilized via technology primarily, a tactic that a 72 year old did not pursue or understand to its fullest. Barack Obama broke the rules because he was playing a different game. As Michael Cornfield highlights in Sabato's book, technology was a "game changer" and Obama knew how to play it. Videos, texting, emails, and blogging help "further political value through their proximity to action tools, such as donating, volunteering, commenting, and sharing," Cornfield observes. The Obama administration capitalized on every opportunity.

Though profuse and relentless in their exploitation of resources, the Obama staff remained meticulous. Volunteers were recruited with high standards of performance. Cornfield records, "Temo Figueroa, a union organizer who served as national field director of the Obama campaign, described "Camp Obama" as follows: Attendees go through a vigorous two to four day program that includes training. These trainings are about building local leaders in the communities and fostering long-term relationships to support our common values." Cornfield quotes Ryan Clay, an Ohio volunteer: "Don't pass the baton to someone until you get someone else running at your speed. It's important for organizers and team leaders to find that point where a new leader is running at the same speed- mentally, physically, time-wise, interest level, desire to win- all those things."

It is obvious that the Obama team fought hard and long to achieve the results they did. They harnessed youthful energy and they accomplished more than many thought possible. The team exceeded expectations and set precedents that will be studied by political campaign managers for decades.

Why did these volunteers commit so much effort and time? They were motivated for various reasons I imagine. Isn't that hope? For some I'm sure it was. As I mentioned earlier, Dr. Shade makes the distinction between hopefulness and hope. Hopefulness is a general positive attitude and openness toward the future. Those whose volunteer commitment did not require them to take risks to see political change probably only experienced hopefulness, not true hope that Obama would be the next President of the United States. As one who stands to gain more from investing more, so do people who expend themselves as compared with the complacent. Without risk taking and truly identifying with Obama, those who were only slightly hopeful would soon fade away. Had McCain won, these slightly hopeful people would have resumed their lives as normal. For people with true hope, it would be a four year countdown until Obama had another shot at their dreams.

Interesting facts:

*Since early 2007, Chris Hughes, cofounder of Facebook, worked for the Obama campaign.

*48% of Obama's campaign funding came from donations of $200 or less. Over 3 million people made private donations to the campaign (equal to the total number of people who gave money to all candidates for president in 2004).

Take Risks

Probably the biggest risk Obama took was breaking fundraising protocol and setting a new precedent of declining public money. Cornfield writes, "In June 2008, Barack Obama became the first nominee to decline public money, after saying he would take it if McCain did. He risked public disapproval for going back on a commitment, and the chance that his donations would shrivel up, leaving him with less than the $85 million guaranteed to him under the public financing system. In announcing his decision, Obama said that the system was broken, that the Republicans routinely 'gamed' it, and would expend 'millions and millions of dollars in unlimited donations' to defeat him." This risk directly connects with Obama's distinguishing promise, that the system is broken and he is going to create a new one.

What was Obama's biggest risk? It was not difficult to promise the end of a war that most people disapproved of. It was relatively easy to toe the Democrat Party line as the democrats stood a better chance of winning, according to most political analysts. It was theirs to lose, more-or-less. However, there must have been numerous risks Obama took in the selection of his staff and team members. Simply by association, people can destroy reputations and quickly undermine what has taken years to build. Ultimately, though, by identifying with the common people and putting his trust in them, Obama risked his fortune with theirs.

The biggest risk taken by Obama's constituents was probably voting for a man with little relevant experience. In part, they were willing to do so because Obama made such great strides to identify with them rather than with the elites, special interest groups, and with other power wielders. They chose someone based on unconventional criteria, but more savvy experts had to be persuaded as well.

The Superdelegates essentially decided the democratic primary. Hillary had them in her pocket for almost the entire race. Obama eventually persuaded them to break with their initial commitment and vote for him using these words: "My strong belief is that if we end up with the most states and the most pledges from the most voters in the country, that it would be problematic for the political insiders to overturn the judgment of the voters." Rather than appeal to the elites, Obama focused their attention on the will of the people. To keep the ball rolling, the Obama administration sought out the most influential popular voices to rally support. "Thanks to a carefully choreographed rollout of endorsements, Obama earned enough delegates on the last day of voting to claim the mantle of presumptive nominee," Sizemore stated.

Identify

All politicians must identify with their constituents it would seem. They can be slightly richer and more educated, but they have to communicate that the interests of the people is the center focus of their administration. When times are tough, though, leaders must work even harder to identify with the masses. CEO's flying to Washington in corporate jets to appeal for financial bailout before a government committee accomplished just the opposite. The Big Three learned their lesson and arrived in automobiles the next time they came with hat in hand.

Juxtaposed Evil Wall Street, as the public viewed it, there was Barack Obama, a man who represented the American demographic-born in the U.S. to a white mother and black father, who grew up in Indonesia and whose roots trace back to Kenya. The USA Today wrote, "To see all the places connected to Obama's life story, you'd have to visit three countries, six time zones and six states. Obama grew up in Hawaii and Indonesia, has roots in Kansas and Kenya, and went to school in Los Angeles, New York and Boston. He and his wife have raised their girls in Chicago" and now they live in Washington DC.

Obama's stories of early days in politics pounding the pavement and eating pies at local diners on his senator campaign trail endeared listeners. Doesn't everyone like pie? Obama was always trying to invoke and involve the public, to mobilize them for change. Cornfield highlights that The "Dinner with Obama" contest connected better than Romney's "make your own ad" and Hillary's "choose a theme song" contests. "Hillary announced the winner of her contest; Obama was seen talking with and listening to the winners of his."

95

Personal touch matters. By embracing Facebook, MySpace, texting, and even announcing his VeeP candidate from his Blackberry, Obama showed he connected with the culture of the present day.

In sync with the hope paradigm, Obama also understood the need to connect with the past. The political analyst Sizemore observes, "Barack Obama accepted the Democratic Party's nomination for president on the final night of the convention, Thursday, August 28, 45 years to the day after Martin Luther King delivered his historic 'I Have a Dream' speech on the steps of the Lincoln Memorial." Obama took Lincoln's 137 mile rail journey from Philadelphia to Washington for his inauguration. He even served as Senator of Illinois, as did Lincoln. It is obvious that Obama deliberately identified himself with this former President. Obama also identified with F.D.R., instituting Fireside Chats, a la YouTube.

The economic comparison between the Great Depression and the 2008 Credit Crisis only solidified Obama's symbolic connection with Roosevelt. Political analysts also compared Obama to John F. Kennedy, as youthful and idealistic. Senator Edward Kennedy believed it, evidenced by his endorsement of Obama. As one of the most respected families in politics. Kennedy's vouch for Obama affected an exchange of inexperience for credibility.

Among Obama's 952 endorsements that Wikipedia records, Warren Buffet and Oprah Winfrey probably boosted his campaign the most. In an economic crisis the recommendation of the most respected billionaire investor is quite powerful. And few would contest that Oprah Winfrey is one of the most influential people in America. Perhaps Hillary Clinton's eventual support did unite the Democratic Party, though. A preliminary conversation happened behind closed doors that might have smoothed Obama's path. Did Hillary strike a deal to be appointed Secretary of State in exchange for rallying her disappointed constituents? Her voice and actions could have hurt the Party as Ross Perot did in 1992 when Bill Clinton won the Presidency. Though slightly unconvincing, Hillary Clinton's endorsement still moved the Democrats forward and those who did not identify with Obama still followed Hillary.

Identification is a symbolic power- one of the greatest forces to drive change. As marketers attest, people only desire what they have seen. Out of sight is out of mind. If people cannot see themselves wearing a fashionable coat and looking good, if they cannot smell the leather, if they cannot anticipate people's compliments and admiration, they will not try it on and they will not buy it. Connect with a person's desires and you win their allegiance. Persuasion is an art. Not only must the communicator identify with his or her audience, the listeners must also connect with the one voicing the message.

Roger Soder's book, *The Language of Leadership,* proposes that a leader's logos, pathos, and ethos combine to effectively persuade an audience. Logos is logic. If the argument is not sound, people will discover the holes and shred it to pieces. Pathos is emotion. If constituents do not experience excitement or anticipation, or if they do not sense that the speaker understands their felt needs, no emotional bond will form. Ethos is ethics. A message can be logical and emotionally compelling but if it does not resonate with the culture's values or elevate the culture's ideals, the messenger will fail to persuade. Obama's language successfully persuaded because he mastered all three and he created the I-Thou relationship of solidarity- shared values, shared vision, and shared fortunes.

The black vote was practically unanimous in favor of Obama, 96 percent. Two-thirds of each demographic group- Latinos, Asian Americans and people ages 18-29, identified with Obama. Seventy three percent of poor Americans making less than $15,000 voted for him. And Obama won 69% of first time voters. John McCain tried to connect with "Joe the Plumbers" of America who make more than $250,000 annually but Obama won the majority of this group as well. Obama had 336 field offices to McCain's 101, a representation of three times the amount of effort Obama's administration made to build relationships with people. McCain ultimately failed to capitalize on the greatest means to build a shared identity- adversity.

Had McCain connected his five years as a prisoner of war with the prisons people live in every day, he might have trumped hope and change with a *freedom* slogan. Obama's negligible personal experience with suffering proved insignificant in that it was eclipsed by the collective suffering slaves endured for centuries. Being black meant Obama carried the suffering hopes of millions with him. People get tired of suffering, though, and they appreciate a little diversion. Obama won the entertainment election hands-down. With all of his appearances on Tonight Shows and conversations with talk show hosts, Obama went to the places where the people go, where the people know your name.

There is no doubt Obama received more publicity and more positive publicity at that. The sketches on Saturday Night Live, with Tina Fey as Sarah Palin, also worked in Obama's favor during the presidential election. Sabato records, however, that only 12% of this information, including broadcasts by the major news networks, actually provided any useful content that helped voters make informed decisions. This only emphasizes that hope, or hype disguised as hope, is more powerful than knowledge. Even so, I disagree that Obama's campaign was all fluff and no stuff. He inspired hope and shaped the American culture.

HOPE

"I have a dream that one day this nation will rise up and live out the true meaning of its creed: 'We hold these truths to be self-evident, that all men are created equal.'"

- Martin Luther King, Jr.

Martin Luther King Jr.'s dream came true on January 20, 2009, Inauguration Day. It is indisputable that from the top-down, African Americans have held every position of power that once only whites possessed. The most powerful position in the world is now held by a black man. The nations rejoiced and celebrated, marking this day a new day, a day when all men and women are recognized as having been *created equal*. Persecutors and racists may remain but a new precedent has been set and a cultural transformation has ensued.

For all the critics who might say that Obama only won because of his race and who emphasize Martin Luther King Jr.'s subsequent exhortation, "I have a dream that my four little children will one day live in a nation where they will *not be judged by the color of their skin* but by the content of their character," may they remember the order to Dr. King's speech- First, all people must be equal. Then, and only then can they be judged by the content of their character!

The Apostle Paul wrote, "Suffering produces perseverance; perseverance, character; and character, hope. And hope does not disappoint us." This verse proposes a macro-view of hope. In the concept of a system, hope is at the end and at the beginning- it is an end that becomes the means to another end. So, if you voted for Obama, you most likely discovered hope somewhere along the way before November 4, 2008, and his victory for you is the means to even greater ends. Consider my definition again:

Hope is orientation and action towards the most meaningful future.

If you engaged your imagination with Obama, what action did you take before the elections? What risks did you take? What did you see in Obama that made you identify with him? When you pinpoint the timing of the answers to those questions you will know at what moment you discovered hope.

Steve Jobs

age 50+

Dealer in hope

Leading Change & Shaping culture:

　From computers to digital life.

　　　Most people either view Steve Jobs as a god or as a tyrant. No matter our personal opinion, Jobs has a lot to teach us about hope and its power to lead change and shape culture. I will say that sometimes Steve Jobs was a dealer in hope and sometimes he was a stealer of hope. He mimicked the leadership style of those who deal in hope but there is one character flaw that hindered him- his obsession with control. Jobs took control of Apple for a second time in 1997, but only in the last five years did he learn that control was no longer as necessary. In fact, Apple's greatest success as of late is in part due to partnership with third-party developers who want access to the iPhone platform.

　　　As much as Apple owes its success to Steve Jobs, many great things have happened in spite of him or simply because of hope's systemic nature. Jobs might be the man who set things in motion but many things have taken on a life of their own. This is the emergent beauty of hope.

Apple was pleasantly surprised by the potential of the iPhone, and rightfully so if one is dealing with authentic hope. As I mentioned, the natural sparkle of hope includes success, satisfaction, and surprise. Apple possesses all three. Perhaps Jobs' intense search for hope's sparkle led to his discovery of how to lead change and shape culture.

I want to walk you through how Jobs led change and shaped culture with a hope paradigm, though perhaps unaware he was doing anything of the kind. In pursuit of the sparkle, Jobs really stumbled into hope more than harnessed it. He was a mastermind of marketing, making his gadgets sparkle, but he was oblivious to the Sparkle's Source.

Jobs dazzled the world by unearthing hope, giving millions a way to create, learn, and entertain. He has been credited with bringing out the best work in some as one engineer attests, remembering how Steve Jobs recruited him- "I hear you're great, but everything you've done so far is crap. Come work for me." But the irony of Jobs' leadership greatness is that he did not know how to develop other great leaders.

Developing leaders is different than getting people to produce and be effective. Empowering others was not his priority and neither was succession planning. At the most recent and last Macworld Expo Apple would ever attend, Jobs pulled a "no show" and his VP of Product Marketing was left without a chair when the music stopped. VP Schiller's presentation underwhelmed in comparison to Jobs' previous performances. Perhaps Jobs thought this man needed no introduction, but "no-confidence" was the message communicated. Many anticipate the demise of Apple now that Jobs is gone, unless a new hope rises.

Jobs' shoes are hard to fill because of his standards of excellence and his relentless pursuit of perfection. Mediocre was unacceptable. Cutting corners to make a profit was abominable. Jobs did not settle for business as usual. Work came out of inspiration and passion, not the pursuit of increased profit margins. Jobs longed for something more- significance, which transcends success. Everything Apple offers today, in products and services, came from Jobs' search for significance (satisfaction).

Satisfaction

Viktor Frankl's experiences in a concentration camp led him to conclude, "...the true meaning of life is to be discovered in the world rather than within man or his own psyche, as though it were a closed system."   In clarifying Maslow's hierarchy of needs which points humans toward self-actualization, Frankl says, "Self actualization is only possible as a side-effect of self-transcendence."   In other words, get over yourself and make life meaningful by encountering other people or by simply creating. Bono of U2 echoes Frankl, that self-discovery is not about "naval gazing."

Steve Jobs' business philosophy was greatly influenced by such soulful artists as Bono. Apple even chose U2 to launch the iPod into the next dimension, featuring a red and black mp3 beauty signed by the band- but I'm talking about something more significant than endorsements. Steve Jobs was a soul searcher and for him, business was about something more than making money. For Jobs, business had to be close to a religious experience.

In talking about the promise of *"America"* Bono said, "It is the land of reinvention. It is never about where you come from, it's always about where you're going...This is the heart of the idea of redemption, to begin again." Jobs would become a master at reinvention in relation to the Apple brand but he first had to set out from America on a more personal, spiritual quest.

As a young man, Jobs went to India to "find himself" but, to his surprise, he was not there to be found. Only when he landed his passions and talents in Cupertino California did Jobs discover self-transcendence was possible. He struggled to mix spirituality and business but when he realized that he could be a karma-capitalist in America, he decided to reinvent himself and the world of business through technological innovation.

This wanderer would not lose his soul for riches or sell-out for success, though. The religious ideals of purity, beauty, simplicity, and devotion are what drove this secular priest who delivered his sermons in black mock turtlenecks to the hope starved masses. His followers hung on his every word and they waited expectantly for anything new their benevolent leader might offer. The benediction of every keynote speech delivered by Jobs began with, "There's one more thing," which was always met with applause and joyous laughter. Then Jobs dazzled his audience with Apple's latest innovation.

Followers were shocked and disappointed when Jobs failed to give the keynote-eulogy at Apple's last Macworld event but he did have some famous last words on his death bed: "Wow," as he gave his last breath. "There is one more thing," it seems. But Jobs ultimately failed to introduce the world to Apple's next great leader.

Surprises

Apple goes to great lengths, even in supply chain logistics, to ensure that customers are pleasantly surprised. When ordering by phone, the sales agent will promise product delivery within 7-10 business days. The customer might expect a shipment on Friday but it arrives on Wednesday, two days early. Their expectations are exceeded and Apple succeeds in satisfying the customer. This hope trick is built-in, a marketing technique that works every time. More impressive than this, though, is how Apple consistently reinvents itself and sets the trends in the digital world.

Some would argue that Microsoft is the industry leader of computer technology and they might be right, but Apple's focus has shifted. In 2007 the company changed its name from Apple Computers Inc. to Apple Inc, and created an entire new industry. In the mid 1990's Jobs witnessed declining market share and perceived Apple's inevitable demise even as the king of the specialty market. The commodity market driven by Microsoft, Dell, and Compaq was bludgeoning Apple with the stick of universal compatibility. Apple could boast a superior operating system but the world worked on Windows and Microsoft Office. Yet, without a serious competitor, business performance dwindles and hegemony hinders innovation.

Bill Gates purchased $150 million of Apple stock and agreed to make Microsoft Office available for the Apple OS. This act probably saved both companies in the late 1990's, one from becoming a monopoly and the other from becoming irrelevant. Tired of resource dependence, Jobs envisioned a new technological future and created the world of digital entertainment and education. Apple's biggest surprise of the early 21st Century would be organizational transformation and the crea-tion of a new industry.

The Organizational Life Cycle proceeds from *birth* to *growth* to *maturity* to *decline* and to *death*, or to <u>*transformation*</u>. For instance, Nokia used to be a lumber company but instead of dying quietly, they transcended and transformed into a cell phone company. Albert Vicere & Robert Fulmer, authors of *Leadership By Design*, suggest that the same phenomenon exists with leadership and observe a direct correla-tion with an organization's orientation to change. In the "emergent" (birth) phase leaders are innovative. As the organization matures, lead-ers take an adaptive approach to change, and as their flexibility stiffens, they become more reactionary. Vicere and Fulmer propose, "In the emergence stage, the style of strategic leadership necessary for organ-izational growth and development is typified by the notion of a prophet. A prophet is a visionary, a zealot driven by an ideal typically embodying a new and different way to deal with the world and some of its opportu-nities." Jobs suited up to fulfill this role.

Apple is a paradox, existing in an emergent, growing, and ma-ture state simultaneously. Jobs was a prophet-leader archetype who forced Apple to constantly innovate. He set the trends and took a lot of risks but his company is very stable. Apple is very mature and fiscally responsible, carrying zero debt and possessing a "war chest," as they say, of around $98 billion. Peter Elkind of Fortune says, "On the brink of bankruptcy when he returned (1997), Apple now has a market value of $108 billion- more than Merck, McDonald's, or Goldman Sachs. $1,000 invested in Apple shares on the day Jobs took over is worth about $36,000 today."

Without Jobs or his leadership style, Apple will likely be headed for decline. Interestingly, VP Schiller did not reveal a new wonder at the last Macworld Expo, perhaps another reason for Jobs' absence. How can a company sustain an annual unveiling of one marvel after another?   Structure was driving strategy and Jobs put an end to it. He would not sacrifice the power of surprise to meet the Expo's deadline.

Innovative surprises are fueled by hope, and a boost of $20 million in R&D as Apple recently did, does not hurt either. This type of investment also protects maturing products. Many have tried to predict the iPod's saturation point, but they failed to understand the platform's potential. On top of music Apple introduced photos and a color screen. Then came video along with photos on top of music. Then came a cell phone along with video, along with photos on top of music. The much-anticipated all-in-one device is almost in the public's hands. With voice recognition and longer battery life, the only thing missing is ubiquitous 4G networks in a wi-fi America.

Google wants to buy the bandwidth once occupied by television and make the United States completely wireless. Unfortunately Apple and Google had a falling out before Jobs died and this may come back to bite Apple unless a new deal can be struck. Imagine the Google Droid phone on a US wifi free network while iPhone users have to sign-up for a subscription plan. Perhaps Apple has another surprise up their sleeve to successfully compete.

Success

Jack Welch, the famous former CEO of GE, nominated Steve Jobs "the most successful CEO today." Elkind states that Jobs has "listed himself 'co-inventor' on 103 separate Apple patents." Notably, Jobs became a multi-millionaire in his early twenties, he bought Pixar from George Lucas for $10 million and sold it to Disney for $7.4 billion, and he battled cancer bravely.

Bono quipped when asked what is the greatest U2 song, "We haven't written it yet." So too, Jobs kept searching for his magnum opus. Not quite a philanthropist, Jobs was generously passionate about education and believed that Apple's goal was to enhance learning through technology.

iTunes U is a breakthrough. Ordinary people can have access to the best and the brightest professors at no cost. To further this, Apple just hired Joel Podolny, Dean of Yale's School of Mangement, to work on a project called Apple University.

It would not be too lofty a dream for Steve Jobs to transform the world's educational system. As Dr. Stout envisions, "Soon professors will be like rock stars." Students will learn from the best at affordable prices because of economy of scale. A classroom will consist of thousands of people logged in to Apple University. This is all speculation, of course, as is every well-guarded secret that entices Apple fans to spawn and spread rumors. The Macdaddy of surprises might surprise us even now that he has gone.

Jobs defined success in his own words (taken from the Commencement address at Stanford University in 2005):

> Don't lose faith. I'm convinced that the only thing that kept me going was that I loved what I did. You've got to find what you love. And that is as true for your work as it is for your lovers. Your work is going to fill a large part

of your life, and the only way to be truly satisfied is to do what you believe is great work. And the only way to do great work is to love what you do. If you haven't found it yet, keep looking. Don't settle. As with all matters of the heart, you'll know when you find it. And, like any great relationship, it just gets better and better as the years roll on. So keep looking until you find it. Don't settle.

For Jobs, success and satisfaction in life were found in doing what you love, doing what you believe is a great work. It does not matter what other people think. Jobs could have cared less about making a profit with his creations, reason enough for being fired in 1985. When he returned in 1997, Jobs realized that making money is important, as long as it does not control you or make decisions for you.

Jobs finished the graduation speech acknowledging the greatest gift to finding hope- death. "Remembering that I'll be dead soon is the most important tool I've ever encountered to help me make the big choices in life. Because almost everything — all external expectations, all pride, all fear of embarrassment or failure - these things just fall away in the face of death, leaving only what is truly important."

Reflecting on what could have been the death of his dream, Jobs said, "I didn't see it then, but it turned out that getting fired from Apple was the best thing that could have ever happened to me." It was then that he realized he still loved what he did and he decided to keep doing it. "The heaviness of being successful was replaced by the lightness of being a beginner again, less sure about everything. It freed me to enter one of the most creative periods of my life." This philosophy on business and life allowed hope to work its magic in his organization, but mysteriously, as Steve would have wanted it.

Think Different. Hope Different

To lead change and shape culture it is first important to make sure a hopescape exists. The environment has to be right before hope can erupt and transformational change can occur.

Adversity

Jobs got fired in 1985 and Apple was almost bankrupt by 1997. Technology faced a great void of innovation right before the tech stock bubble burst.

Voice

What do people want?   Jobs has been considered the expert with the answer to that question.

#1 "Give me something that works":   Leander Kahney, author of *The Cult of Mac,* quotes a Mac user, "Portraying Mac people as zealots is a way to minimize the fact that the Mac is a more advanced system. Actually, looking at the software and hardware combinations available, one realizes that people are dedicated to Macintosh because it just works."   Simply put, people want a product they can count on. Case in point, viruses don't just kill computers, they kill people's incentive to buy PCs. Apple products are known to be more intuitive and reliable.

#2 "Stick it to the man": Kahney writes, "To Mac users, Apple represents everything that Microsoft isn't. Apple innovates; Microsoft copies. Apple puts out solid products; Microsoft represents business and conformity. Apple is the scrappy underdog; Microsoft is the big, predatory monopoly." People innately rebel against conformity.

#3 "Think different": People want to be creative and unique. Marketer Marc Gobé, an expert on branding, says of companies like Apple, "People are drawn to these brands because they are selling their own ideas back to them, they are selling the most powerful ideas that we have in our culture, such as transcendence and community." Kahney comments on one specific Apple ad with the logo juxtaposed Che Guevara and the tag line: Think Different: "The '1984' ad began a branding campaign that portrayed Apple as a symbol of counter-culture-rebels, free-thinking, and creative."

Promises

The television ad "Think Different" released in 1997, now on YouTube, begins, "Here's to the crazy ones, the misfits, the rebels, the troublemakers, the round pegs in the square holes, the ones who see things differently. They're not fond of rules and they have no respect for the status quo..." The pictures that flash on the screen are all types of people who deal in hope or are agents of transformational change. Since people want to be original, creative, and use their talents to make the world a better place, they identify with the ad. Apple promises to give them the tools they need to do just that. Apple partners with these people and imagines a meaningful future together with them.

Imagination

Along with the idea of "Think Different" is the simplicity of the Mac- a broad platform for the human imagination. The computers are designed to be open space for creative work. Apple's winning formula is: Give people the tools they need, make the creative process intuitive and non-cumbersome, and let people express themselves uniquely, the way they want to. Mac computers appeal to trend setters, like musicians and artists who want a place to create. The iPhone is a platform for people to express their imaginations and the most creative and practical innovations make money there. It is a solid business model to protect intellectual capital.

Steve Jobs is not only transforming the economics of business, he is creating a new model for education. Business has evolved and so has Apple. Education has not but Apple will see that it does.

Business evolution:

products $\longrightarrow$ services $\longrightarrow$ experiences $\longrightarrow$

interactive development

Most companies do not have the luxury of simply making products. They have to provide on-going services that people want. For instance, Apple Care is a great support service for people, especially those unfamiliar with Mac products. Jobs knew this was not enough so he created more access points to engage customers. Mac Stores are a wonderland of technology. It is a neat, clean, streamlined experience where live tech support people, i.e. geniuses, give tours through Apple-topia. Apple is now even offering application development training for people interested in selling their product or service through the iPhone.

This cooperative-interactive development aspect of business allows people to partner and create with the company. Gaming and so-cial networking sites like Second Life are moving in this direction as well. Education, on the other hand, has remained the same didactic product for the most part.

iTunes U is still very primitive, but it is a start. Presently, its only major advantage over traditional learning is mobility. Apple is moving forward along a wiki-track, though, where collaboration can enhance learning. They left the computer industry for the world of digital enter-tainment & education with an emphasis on mobility and interaction but it has been a long row to hoe and Jobs wasn't always so patient.

Jobs was the "imagination run wild." However, Jobs almost strangled Apple and shut down the creative factory because of his need for control. Being fired might have been the greatest thing that ever happened to Apple and to Jobs, who himself was out of control. He was a ball-hog, always taking the credit for good ideas and making others feel like mental midgets in his presence. This was before 1997. Wan-dering in the wilderness for ten years sobered him and when he re-turned to Apple, he returned as a team-player- like the new Michael Jordan when he played under Phil Jackson and won six NBA Champi-onships. Before that Jordan scored almost twice as much but he never empowered his team to win big. Teamwork and working with a good team make all the difference.

Teamwork

Up until 1997 no one thought of Jobs as a team player. But exile can change a man. Jefferey Young and William Simon, authors of *iCon Steve Jobs: the Greatest Second Act in the History of Business*, cover this behavioral one-eighty in detail. "...Steve Jobs was back- and not just back, but with a vengeance, as chief executive. His first suggestion was to re-price stock options so that staff morale would improve; his second, to make everyone in the company work for a bonus that was stock-related so the whole crew would pull together." This is a very good tactical approach that instills hope. Link everyone's destiny. As the Declaration of Independence says, "...we pledge to each other our Lives, our Fortunes, and our sacred Honor."

Jobs did not set the bar quite as high as did the Forefathers but he did announce that all Apple people are created equal. "He set out on an egalitarian remake of Apple. No more business-class travel. No more sabbaticals. No more special severance deals for executives. Everybody in the company was going to be in the same boat," Young and Simon observed. Interestingly, Jobs only took a $1 salary, linking his fortunes with the stock price of the company. This was a captain that was going down with the ship, if need be. Like Ghengis Khan who shattered the status quo and assigned political power to the poor after he killed the ruling rich, Jobs accepted the resignation of most of the board of directors who opposed him. Team would be an inclusive "we" as long as people understood Jobs' role as the Royal 'we'.

Shared values and shared vision meant thinking like Jobs. Employees could "Think Different" as long as they were connected to Steve's brain. Alignment was the key. It seems, though, that as the years passed, wisdom opened Steve's eyes more to what was truly important. Being a father changed his world. Living on death's doorstep gave him perspective. The change was real. Steve's transformation was his greatest achievement.

"Steve in no longer an emperor who stands at the water's edge and demands that the river change its course to his command. He is now the captain on a river hurtling down the rapids; he's guiding the boat, but he has a team of compadres with oars as well. Whether they are animators at Pixar or a thousand software engineers at Apple, Steve is the leader but now understands that he isn't the only important participant.

No one has changed more than he has. In a world of baby boomers who grew to maturity in the sixties and the seventies, he is now an emblem of hope in a complex world. Maybe we aren't encased in an immutable prison by the age of thirty. Maybe we can change for the better."

Team work means we're all in this boat together. So let's be real, let's be passionate, and "let's be pirates," as Jobs said to inspire his idealistic engineer types. Take a geek and make him an outlaw instead of an outcast, that is how you inspire your team to take risks and achieve.

Take Risks

It is almost completely unnecessary to talk about Apple and Steve Jobs on the subject of taking risks. The two are considered a magic combination for creativity, the envy of others who only hope to be 1/10th as innovative. So, let me mention two products that were "before their time," so to speak, as examples of Apple's willingness to push the envelope and even fail. The Macbook Air and AppleTV were perhaps 3-5 years premature, in terms of what the public needed, wanted, and could adapt to. It is not that these products have such a steep learning curve, they just assumed a different life-style, new work habits, or work-flow, as they say.

People suffer from "future shock." Future shock was a term coined by Alvin Toffler in 1970 to describe people's frustration with technology. People struggle to adapt to the pace of technological change. Do you Facebook? Do you Twitter? What's trending now? You better know or you will be left behind, and being left behind is a lonely feeling. So get with it or we'll find someone who can text in their sleep. That's how people feel when innovation outpaces their ability to learn.

You might feel like an air-head if you cannot appreciate the Macbook Air, which has no disc drive, by the way. Where do you put the DVD to load a new program or watch a movie? You are expected to download programs off the internet. You are expected to watch all movies online, via iTunes or NetFlix. There is a thing called the "cloud" which is where you are expected to store all your documents, pictures, and videos. This cloud is online. If you are off-line, you are screwed. Do not ever go off-line or you will die. If you must, buy an external ROM drive to do things the old way. This is the Macbook Air experience.

Probably only 1% of people live like this- an always online existence. AppleTV works in a similar manner. You are expected to download all movies from the internet and watch them on your gargantuan flat-screen.

TV shows are now all uploaded for people to watch online so why pay for TV on top of the internet at home. Apple saw this coming. They are thinking 5-15 years into the future. So, from time to time they will put out a product that does not connect with your life. Most of it does, though, so the company can eat its failures.

AppleTV might die but it will be resurrected by Samsung or Sony. Apple tried to beat television to the market but why have a separate box when you can put the technology inside the TV? Apple should have partnered with someone like LG and offered exclusive rights to the technology, like they did the iPhone with AT&T. But who am I to say what the King of Silicon Valley should have done? I don't want to be a critic. Jobs left his critics in his wake. He lived as the "man in the arena," as Teddy Roosevelt would say, and he invited others to come out of the stands and get bloody too.

Identify

Among the most loyal customers of any brand, Apple fans have to be the most extreme. Perhaps Harley-Davidson or Starbucks boast equal devotion, but few tout their pride as much as Mac users. PC users often ask Mac people, "So, do you like your Mac?" Responses vary- "I love it." "I never have any problems with it." "I'm so glad I switched." "Once you go Mac, you never go back."

Mac users never ask people lugging a PC, "Hey, do you like it?" They are simply mystified that people are still using bulky, virus infected machines. The definition of insanity is "do what you have always done and expect different results," and Mac users think PC users are insane. Mac users feel sorry for people whose job makes them use a PC. It's more sympathy these days than an air of superiority, though. After the success of the iPod, a vindication of sorts for Mac enthusiasts, Mac users have relaxed and now simply make fun of PCs instead of PC users.

The ad campaign, "Hi, I'm a Mac. And I'm a PC" took the concept of "identify" to its natural extreme- You are what you use. The Mac person highlighted all their superior features and essentially made Mr. PC look dumb, in a funny, playful sort of way. Mac users love the commercials and now PC users have something to hate about Apple. The roles have reversed. There is Mac envy.

Microsoft, in true form, showed its lack of creativity once again by copying Apple in their reactionary ad which accepts the nomenclature, "I'm a PC... ." Instead of defining their own identity, Microsoft kept the nickname that had already stuck and tried to spin it to make PC users feel good about themselves. Instead of slandering their competition, PC people simply expressed their pride in what they do and how they work with PC technology. Now PCs look like a martyr because they have accepted the abuse without apology and refuse to recant their identity.

Christians are a great example of the martyrdom phenomenon. They were persecuted and killed up until 313 A.D. when the Roman Emperor Constantine declared an edict of tolerance. Subsequently, Christianity began to grow in popularity and in 380 another Emperor recognized it as the official religion of the Roman Empire. The word

Christian is actually a derogatory term, though, first spoken to mock people who thought they were like Jesus. Christian means, "little Christ," a name to poke fun at people for identifying with the Jewish leader.

The surprising thing about persecution and martyrdom is that it has quite the opposite effect than what is Intended. Instead of people withdrawing and renouncing their beliefs, they identify even more with the movement. Every sacrifice only enables people to identify more with those who have suffered before them. A martyr embodies the ideals of the people and their death only stirs up the followers who refuse to let those ideals die as well.

Which computer or cell phone you use to type an email to your boss is hardly a life or death issue, but the principle of identity is what we are after here. For years Apple users had to prove their system was better than Windows. With the success of different products like the iPod and iPhone, Macs have gained credibility by association.

The more prevalent Apple products become, the less fanatical the followers will be. In the new industries of digital entertainment and education, Apple will have to figure out new ways for people to identify with the Apple culture. Right now, though, as long as Apple echoes the voice of the people (the three things I listed earlier), Apple products will gain in market share. More and more people are identifying with Apple as the leader in a new industry because people want to go where Jobs was leading them. They had hope that he would take them into a meaningful future.

Hope

It is obvious that Steve Jobs was addicted to hope. He understood adversity as meaningful. He heard the voice of the people, perhaps even the voices of those calling back to him from the future. His promise was simple- Apple will devote itself to improving the quality of life through technology. While possessing a healthy discontentment with the status quo and yet able to celebrate achievements and live in the moment, Jobs balanced the "now and not yet" very well. He realized that the future is connected to the past and the present, the holistic perspective that makes room for hope to grow. Jobs learned to be a team player. He wanted to leave a legacy and he knew he could not do this with a focus on himself.

You would think that Jobs has already made it into technology's Hall of Fame but the thrill of technology is fleeting. If technology changes every seven seconds and the change is accelerating, how long will it be before Jobs is listed 273 on a google search of technology innovators?   He knew technology would eclipse him, so his legacy would not be the next great innovation.

Jobs' legacy will probably be connected to his successor who builds on Jobs' foundation. Jobs' love for music found expression in iTunes and the iPod. His love for dynamic education is finding expression in iTunes U and Apple University. His love seems to be contagious.

I recently spoke with a high school student holding in her arms a book about Steve Jobs. I asked her why she was reading it. She replied, "I love Steve Jobs. I love Apple." Perhaps Jobs' legacy is wrapped up in 'doing what you love.' Love might be as contagious as hope. It seems that they work well together, love, faith, and hope.

Even though he did not finish college, Jobs had an insatiable love for learning and teaching. He even learned to respect his own limitations. As surprising as that might sound, hope has a healthy, humble perspective regarding individual limitations, which forces us to learn and then create out of that new knowledge. This took Jobs many years to understand but his supernova in the last few years, which dwarfs his microbursts of the prior thirty, definitely reflects this quality of hope.

Technology depends on "break-through" and Progress. Jobs initially wanted to control the process, but in the end hope taught him that some things come at you that you did not anticipate, which makes life better than we expected it could be. The lesson is- leave room for surprises. Steve Jobs will not go down in history as the world's greatest innovator, but as a 'dealer in hope' who shaped global culture.

Mike Morhaime

age 40+

Dealer in hope

Leading Change & Shaping Culture:

 New cultural reality, mixture of the "real" and the virtual.

　　　Most likely the name Mike Morhaime does not ring a bell. He is the CEO of a gaming company called Blizzard Entertainment. Their website reads, "Blizzard Entertainment® is a premier developer and publisher of entertainment software. After establishing the Blizzard Entertainment label in 1994, the company quickly became one of the most popular and well-respected makers of computer games." In 2004 Blizzard launched World of Warcraft (WoW). This game is the most popular online video game, boasting more than eleven million monthly members

worldwide - 2011. This is a major accomplishment in the virtual and cor-
responding "real" world.

World of Warcraft is referred to as a MMORPG (massively multiplayer online role-playing game). Do not think Monopoly; think of a
video game where a person from Brazil can play with someone from
Chicago, if they are on the same computer server. Morhaime's world
consists of many continents and many races, a mythical place of elves,
taurens, trolls, gnomes, dwarves, orcs, humans and NPCs (non-player
characters). An NPC is any computer character not controlled by a person outside the game and usually a target, a point of reference, or part
of a game objective. The mythology helps create an alternate reality.

There is a story line that some players follow, basically a plot of
good against evil. There are quests, or objectives players pursue to
achieve various rewards- including economic, political and personal
advancement. Winning is a relative concept but reaching the highest
level, currently level 85, and defeating the most evil character is considered "beating the game." There are rules, like with any game, and
with the momentum of such unprecedented success, Morhaime's company seems to be creating new rules for the real world as well.

Mike Morhaime has won numerous awards for the development
of this virtual world. In CNN's *50 People Who Matter Now*, Morhaime is
ranked 46. Oprah Winfrey 38, Bill Gates 21, and Steve Jobs 5. Interestingly, "YOU" (the consumer as creator) is ranked number one. This reflects the transformation of many industries, including gaming, which
has also adopted collaborative product and service development. Morhaime encourages "addons," or third party software programs as they
enhance game play in World of Warcraft. Many members have voluntarily created support websites as well. Inspiring this kind of participa-

tion is key to leading change and in the final chapter I will discuss how "YOU" can achieve this with a hope paradigm.

Why does Morhaime "matter" so much in the business world? One reason is that in 2008 gaming entertainment was a $21 billion industry which grew over 20% from the previous year and WoW possesses over 60% of the online market. The gaming market is undiscovered country, so to speak, a local-global place open 24 hours a day, 365 days a year. This virtual access to the whole world makes globalization look easy. Morhaime essentially blazed the trail into this alternative reality, proving the world is not flat and neither is it round. It is malleable, like silly putty. If I live on the edge of this world, I can flip the contour to touch another place and create a new, shared space. Someone living in New York can dig a hole to China, more-or-less. Mongolia could be as real to me as Massachusetts. This new reality essentially shrinks space to fit onto a computer or cell phone screen and thereby expands new business potential.

Morhaime has gathered eleven of the 360 million people on the internet Into his world, making Blizzard Entertainment a billion dollar company. This is astounding success but perhaps minute in comparison to the effect he has had on culture. Whether or not you are among the 69% of Americans who play computer and video games and whether or not you have experienced the space where the virtual becomes real, Mike Morhaime and his World of Warcraft have a lot to teach us about hope.

To outsiders this new reality might seem like a world of despair rather than hope, but Morhaime is leading many people to an oasis, not a mirage. Outside observers, whether family, friends, or coworkers, accuse some WoW players of being addicted to the game. If ten hours a week playing time is considered average, pulling an all-nighter might seem obsessive, especially when the player falls asleep at work the next day. Friends of mine who live closer to the corporate world in New York City have told me that employers discourage WoW membership because of the game's reputation as an all-consuming influence in a person's life. There are many sociological and psychological reasons for this type of behavior but I believe hope is at the core. People are addicted to hope.

You might argue that the virtual world only offers virtual hope, not the real hope for true change. You might think that games are meaningless outside of having a little fun or daily diversion. Yet, people will pay real money, US currency, to buy WoW gold that enables them to purchase weaponry or transportation in the game. Second Life is another online world that has blurred the virtual and the real. People pay real money to buy virtual real estate, or would that be virtual estate, and the figures as of 2009 showed that sixteen acres rented for around $320/mo. People mix the two worlds and create new shared places, new worlds for others to discover.

This is the major change Morhaime has helped lead- people now value the virtual as an overlay to the real which essentially creates a new reality. The world works differently in World of Warcraft because there are different rules (values). Some would say it is a fairer world. The modern philosopher McKenzie Wark proposes that some online games reflect the more perfect world humans are trying to create.

There is a running joke in online dating, that people exaggerate their physical features to appear more attractive. The dilemma, however, comes at the first real encounter. If we reject someone on sight when we really enjoyed them online, does this mean that in the "real" world we are shallower people?

By now most of us know a couple that met online and are either dating or got married. So first virtual encounters are effective enough to lead to real relationships. Even so, you may not like this new way of dating or that online gaming is a new context for community, perhaps even the future of education. Suspend your feelings for a moment to take a look inside Morhaime's world where hope is alive and empowering people to lead change and shape culture for the better. Remember, the hopescape to lead change requires an element that seems threatening to the formation of hope- adversity.

Adversity- "Agon"

Agon is the ancient Greek word for contest or competition. Games are mostly about competition. Agon is the very real context for capitalism as well. Companies compete for customer loyalty and referrals, to be first to market, to win investor support, and for talent. It is a system designed around agony. Your work may seem agonizing as opposed to fun or entertaining, and you might envy others who say they enjoy what they do, but not even those people can avoid the struggle, the adversity, the hardships of work. The ancient Jewish scriptures suggest that when Adam and Eve broke trust with God, the Lord put a curse on work as a punishment. Work would forever be "painful toil."

Humans have always tried to make work easier but there is no escape from the unending labor to ensure survival. A privileged few make their money work for them instead of working for money, but even these people must manage their wealth or they will lose it. Most of us have met someone who "never did a hard day's work in their life," and we might envy them, but we look down on them too. They have not suffered and therefore they do not deserve the comfort or the rewards that come from achievement. Humans resist and yet thrive on "agon."

In the landmark movie, *the Matrix,* evil Agent Smith describes how the machines created the fake human world, the Matrix. While interrogating Morpheus, the leader of the human rebellion, Agent Smith reveals that the matrix is actually the machine's second version of reality. He explains:

"Have you ever stood and stared at it (the matrix)? Marvelled at its beauty? Billions of people, just living out their lives, oblivious. Did you know that the first Matrix was designed to be a perfect human world? Where none suffered, where everyone would be happy. It was a disaster. No one would accept the program, entire crops were lost. Some believed that we lacked the programming language to describe your perfect world. But I believe, that as a species, human beings define their reality through misery and suffering."

Is that true? Is suffering essential to how humans live and work? It seems that people only appreciate what they work for, when they overcome obstacles to achieve their goals. Ironically, technology is a human attempt to eradicate "agon," but it has been an agonizing maturity process to develop technology.

The more technology has advanced, the more game-like the real world seems. The U.S. Military practices "War Games" to formulate strategies for different scenarios that might evolve in battle. Fighter pilots learn through simulation (video games) and real bombs are dropped by drones- miniature planes controlled from computer screens. Death and destruction look different on a computer screen than when it is up-close and in-person, though. It's not hard to understand that the lines of reality are quickly blurred when actions taken in the virtual world impact the "real" world.

McKenzie Wark, author of Gamer Theory, proposes the metaphor that life is a game. "Work is a rat race. Politics a horse race. The economy is a casino," Wark says. At first the idea seems cynical and negative, but Wark is teaching his readers to be critical thinkers, even if they are inside the game of life where "every action is just a means to an end" and "all that counts is the score." Wark quotes the Italian philosopher Paolo Virno, "At the base of contemporary cynicism is the fact that men and women learn by experiencing rules rather than 'facts'." In other words, some rules in life are often more important than the related facts and this can seem unfair, e.g., promotions based on relational ties rather than excellent performance.

Life as a game could be meaningless, an "atopia," or worse yet, an ill-fated reality from which there is no escape but, then again, maybe not. At the end of Wark's chapter titled "Agony," the reader does feel slightly hopeless, but I believe this is meant to shake people from their acceptance of the status quo. We only discover hope through agony.

People are willing to suffer for a good cause, but if the rules of the game do not reward perseverance, morale drops and cynicism creeps into the culture. That is why people must be free to critique the "game" and establish better rules.

Blogging as Voice

The internet gives voice to the masses and impacts every facet of culture, unlike the era of newspaper, radio and television which controlled who could broadcast their message. In 2006 "bloggers" won Time Magazine's *Person of the Year*. The internet levels the playing field. YouTube's tag line is "Broadcast Yourself." Random videos get hundreds of thousands of hits because of social networks and word of mouth advertising. The blogger's voice, whether through type or video, once again returns power to the people.

Mike Morhaime and the designers of WoW might be the gods who make the rules of the game, but players have freedom of speech and an open platform to improve the reality where they gather. Within the game itself, there are different chat-lines of communication, which serve their unique purposes. There is a general line, a trade line, a party line, a line to speak with someone privately called "whisper" and a direct line to game experts if you need help. Profanity is unacceptable but otherwise people are free to express themselves on any topic ranging from the death of Michael Jackson to frustrations adults experience playing with snotty kids who do not hesitate to disrespect them in the virtual world. My guild (a more permanent team) only allows adult members for this reason. A world within a world was created in response to an unpleasant reality.

The chat lines allow people to voice what they do not like and collaborate to overcome those unpleasantries. If enough people say, "It sucks walking through the Eastern Kingdoms," then Blizzard Entertainment knows how they need to improve game-play, by offering animals for characters to ride once they reach a certain level. WoW designers also realize that WoW players like diversity and distinguishing them-selves from other players, so they created unique mounts for characters to ride, but they must be earned.

In a way, the members who subscribe to play WoW online are not only customers, they are also shareholders who have invested great amount of time in understanding this virtual world. I just down-loaded an "addon" (third party program) to help me prosper more from the economic system in WoW. Many items are sold via an auction house and the "addon" reads the market prices more efficiently so that I do not lose out by overpricing or underpricing items I have posted for sale. A player voluntarily created that program to improve reality and Blizzard heard their voice. They welcomed the critique and opened their system to accept the program. Voices have been heard, promises have been made, and a hopescape has been created.

Quests as Promises

World of Warcraft is designed around promises. Every quest a player accepts is a promise to reward their character with loot or knowl-edge, provided they pass the test. The elaborate yet simple incentive system in WoW makes playing fun and interesting. Unlike the real world, all promises are kept. However, players' expectations of what should be promised increases, not as a form of entitlement, but as if to say, "Challenge me, I'm ready to face tougher obstacles."

Questing offers characters more than gold and finer weaponry or armor. Accomplishing a quest grants increased experience, improved reputation with different races, and personal satisfaction for having per-severed and overcome the challenge.

WoW has developed a built-in positive peer pressure community where complete strangers will take time to help each other succeed and complete quests. In WoW, characters can even share their quests with others as an incentive for cooperative play. Both characters are rewarded. How unlike the corporate image where one person often steals the glory for another's work! In WoW both personal achievement and collaboration are highly valued.

Leaders must cultivate an environment, whether virtual or real, where people are recognized and rewarded because their behavior reflects the organization's stated values. If a company says it values innovation, but punishes people for taking risks, then hidden rules determine reality. In Morhaime's World of Warcraft there are rules which determine game-play, but cultural values greatly impact player interaction too. One such value is made explicit by Mike Morhaime and the leaders at Blizzard Entertainment: Purchasing WoW gold on eBay or other sites with real money is not against the rules but is looked down upon.

It is hard to acquire gold in World of Warcraft and it could take twenty hours or more before a character accumulates enough copper and silver to equal one piece of gold. Paying three dollars for 1000 gold is a short-cut that destroys the cultural fabric of the game, making things uneven to favor the affluent. That's how the real world works- the rich get richer. In WoW, every player has to put in their time. In the real world people who play the game acquire knowledge of the virtual world through experience, by logging many hours in exploration. Without the agony of overcoming all the obstacles each level offers, a person cannot imagine how to make this virtual world better, and never discover hope.

Avatars- Identity & Imagination

Some people value books over television because the written word allows them to use their imagination more. I admit that I do not want my daughter to watch Lord of the Rings before she reads the books because there is a rich experience for the mind in reading that cinema cannot provide. Some might argue that constant visual stimulation hinders the imagination and therefore online gaming could dull the mind. Admittedly, World of Warcraft leaves little to the imagination in terms of scenery and non-player character appearances. After a while you realize that the higher-level enemies are just bigger versions of the lower level ones.

In effort to overcome the monotony of waging war, the designers have woven mini story lines into the game. Sometimes a quest is as simple as "go kill 10 spiders," but other times you have to speak with four or five non-player characters to learn a tale and discover the secrets that lead to special items. In these unique quests players begin to imagine their role in the game. Image becomes linked with identity, as in the hope paradigm.

The most important imagining a player does involves his or her avatar. An avatar is a digital representation of the creators imagination. Avatars- an Indian religious term for the manifestation of a god in human form, represent a new identity. In the virtual world people create avatars for different social networking sites and for games usually. In WoW, choosing your avatar is an important decision that determines how you will play the entire game. Each race has their strengths and their weaknesses, their advantages in battle, and their strategic role in group play.

The avatar starts out almost naked and has to buy or loot clothing, armor, weapons, and even adornments such as rings and necklaces at the higher levels. This is similar to starting at the bottom of a company and working your way up the corporate ladder. Sometimes you get a break, like when a complete stranger offered me 20 gold so I could buy a horse to ride. She sympathized with the difficulty of playing the game at my level and having to run around everywhere, quite a time consuming process. Also, like in the real world, your avatar's transportation is a status symbol.

Part of the draw to WoW is creating an identity for your avatar. Earning a good reputation, finding matching armor, brandishing a kickass sword, walking around with a wild beast you have tamed to be your pet allows you to be new and different everyday. It is all positive personal development.

In the real world who wouldn't enjoy getting stronger, smarter, slimmer, more important everyday? However, human accomplishment in the real world takes a lot more time, discipline, and is checkered with failure. In WoW, the closest thing to failure is when your character dies and you have to resurrect them.

Similar to a real world situation, I experienced failure in the game because I could not buy a horse at the level most people obtain theirs. I failed to learn my profession early on and I suffered the consequences. My friendliness in the game, however, won me the 20 gold I needed, in part. I struck up the conversation with that player. I offered to help them with one of their quests. I put my best foot forward with this character who was only two levels higher than me. What I did not realize is that she had another level 72 character (you are allowed up to 15 but only one can play at a time). She logged out, logged in as her 72 character, sent 20 gold to her lower level character, logged out, logged in as the character I had met and gave me the 20 gold. Simple as that, right?

I enjoy seeing my avatar become robust and dangerous. As a warrior class I equip my character to wage war powerfully and quickly Some choose to build their warrior to be a "tank," nearly indestructible, but they do not kill as quickly. Some people enjoy checking-out the accomplishments and the gear of other people. Level 80s seem to sit around a lot in major cities and hold elite parties, so to speak. Usually congregating with members of the same guild, these characters are models, heroes, icons of what lower level players want to look like and achieve. It might be rare that a level 80 will talk to a low level character, much like corporate executives and mid-level managers, but sometimes they will share their vast knowledge if you are polite.

Teamwork

As I write this, I am currently a level 36. I joined up with another player two levels higher than me recently and he invited his level 80 friend to join us. We decided to run what is called an "instance." Imagine a hundred enemies, elite status, very powerful, and prone to attack in mobs. We sat and watched as the level 80 character demolished 6 to 15 enemies at a time and then we picked up the loot left in his wake. It took us thirty minutes to run that instance. Had it just been myself and the other level 38, it would have been impossible or taken hours to complete. The level 80 is like our big brother, someone we admire and aspire to be like.

If these kind of imagination and identifying experiences existed in the real business world, companies would double their innovation and production levels. If corporate executives would roll up their sleeves and work an afternoon with mid-level managers, people would be inspired to grow and become a greater asset to the guild, I mean the company.

Perfect teamwork does not exist in WoW either, however. When I was at level 25 I ran my second instance, a dungeon. I recruited four other characters, each with a specific strength, so we could dominate without dying. Two of the people I knew, having played with them before. My friend recruited one player, and the fourth I recruited at the last minute because he happened to be near the dungeon. Even though this last minute recruit was the same level as me, it was obvious his knowledge and experience trumped mine. I yielded to his leadership because of his apparent competence. Big mistake. Just because someone is knowledgeable in a subject does not make them a good leader. This is a common mistake in the corporate world today. We must realize that leadership is almost another profession entirely.

Things went smoothly at first as we killed dozens of prisoners and insurgents in the dungeon, but I was not paying attention to the chat lines. Two characters were arguing. The last recruit, to whom I had deferred, was forcing out another player by taking over his role. He tried to control everything and ended up annoying people in the process. One player quit and then the leader made a bold move without communicating with the team. Enemies swarmed us and most of us died, including the leader. He then typed in the party chat line that he had run the instance before and he did not want to do it again, so he abandoned us. Another player quit and I was left with one friend. The instance was too difficult for just the two of us, so we had to call it a day.

I logged out that night frustrated with the leader who had sabotaged our team, but more so with myself for lacking the knowledge to lead well. However, I learned important lessons about strategic alliances, recruiting, and communication. Teamwork is an art and good leadership an essential role to ensure teams function effectively. My WoW team had failed to imagine- failed to communicate what role each of us would play and what strategy would be the most effective to overcome the challenges before us. Players took risks before the team had clearly articulated a vision, with the false assumption that we all shared the same purpose. The leader violated personal values and failed to make promises that would win him trust. Needless to say, we never discovered hope.

Risk Taking

Maybe the stakes are not high in the virtual world and therefore failure is more palatable. It is easy to risk death all day long when you can easily resurrect. So what risk taking is there in Morhaime's world that could lead people to discover true hope that drives change? Inside the World of Warcraft there is almost zero real risk taking. However, using the habits and skills learned in WoW, people will risk relationships and business deals in the virtual world that are quite real.

In a way, World of Warcraft is a virtual University. There exists a movement called "serious gaming" that abstracts lessons from interactive play. Harvard Business Review recently published an article on leadership development via massively multiplayer online games. The article mentions a study done by Seriosity, a company contracted by

IBM to observe the real impact online games have in management development. The results proved relevant. Some findings were surprising:

> "A number of our conclusions about the future of business leadership were unanticipated. For one, individuals you'd never expect to identify—and who'd never expect to be identified—as "high potentials" for real-world management training end up taking on significant leadership roles in games. Even more provocative was our finding that successful leadership in online games has less to do with the attributes of individual leaders than with the game environment, as created by the developer and enhanced by the gamers themselves. Furthermore, some characteristics of that environment- for example, immediate compensation for successful completion of a project with non-monetary incentives, such as points for commitment and game performance- represent more than mere foreshadowing of how leadership might evolve."

New Reality

Leadership development has focused on psychology and personal styles throughout the last decade. But in the coming years philosophy and sociology must be emphasized. As the HBR article says, environmental conditions are of extreme importance, perhaps more so than typical leadership traits.

Mike Morhaime's World of Warcraft broaches traditional themes like politics, economics, and business practices in the context of social networking and gaming but there is so much more across the virtual sea. Morhaime teaches us how to motivate volunteers to invest and contribute towards a better reality. His world is so great, people are paying to join. If life is a game, why not make it as enjoyable as WoW?

The real world and WoW are both somewhat monotonous but Morhaime overcomes this with constant creation. There are always new lands to discover, new weapons to wield, and new friends to make. Your avatar is constantly transforming too. These surprises hidden around every corner draw millions of people to play and to even contribute beyond the game. People are inspired to create and improve the virtual world. These people have surpassed level 80- they are at the hope level.

Mike Morhaime created the environment where people could discover hope in the virtual and real worlds. He has helped us understand the new reality that has evolved from blending both of these worlds. It is now up to us and our avatars to decide how we will contribute to making the worlds better places.

To Parents

This book is written for professional folks but you are parents too. So let's get practical in this part of your life. Morhaime's world and those similar to it, could help teenagers adapt to the complexity of multiple worlds. In these transitional and transformative years, I wish high schools offered a 101 course in "reality" as part of a required computer class. The lines of reality are blurred and teens are suffering from the effects of duality- being one thing in person and another online.

As I have experienced working with teenagers for over a decade, their greatest struggle is defining who they are. They have little self-confidence and they are stressed from trying to understand reality as they become more self-aware. Representing themselves online is difficult because it gives them a freedom for semi-anonymous expression which distances them from real consequences for their virtual actions. Discovering their "real" identity, let alone a virtual identity, as well as a blended person is quite overwhelming. One sign of this is "sexting." Teenagers would never take off their clothes in public but "sexting" nude pictures in a text message is gaining popularity. Adolescents need an environment where they can experiment in a positive way.

Morhaime's world is a safe place to play and figure these things out. A hope perspective will help young minds discover who they are. I suggest diving into the virtual world with your kids in either a game format or through other social networks.

Moses

60+

Dealer in hope

Leading Change & Shaping culture (FAILURE):

Failure to lead Israelites into the Promised Land.

Everyone Fails

Moses is respected in three religions Judaism, Islam, and Christianity; no small accomplishment. Hundreds of millions of people acknowledge his amazing leadership achievement in delivering the Jews out of slavery from Egypt. Whether you believe the supernatural events recorded transpired or not, Moses has a lot to teach us about hope and more specifically about the impossible task of leading people and shaping culture without hope. Moses is credited with leading his people out of Egypt, but what of his failure to lead the same people into the Promised Land? The Old Testament records that God more-or-less fired Moses and told him that his successor would complete the journey into Canaan. However, as a mature visionary leader, Moses still wanted a glimpse of his people's future. In the last days of his life he climbed a mountain on the approaching side of the Jordan River to see the Promised Land he would never enter.

Like many mythic-based legends about heroes, Moses initially ran and hid from his destiny. Moses tried to convince Yahweh that he was not the man for the job, but God insisted and Moses courageously obeyed. There is speculation about how many Jews left Egypt in the mass exodus but a conservative estimate would be around 2 million people. Imagine how difficult it must have been to mobilize that many in addition to their belongings, their animals, and all the bounty the Egyptians gave to them on their way out. Imagine trying to communicate to the masses without technology. Everything was verbal. What a leadership challenge that must have been!

How many people are there in your organization? I'm sure trying to get them all to move in the same direction is quite a feat even with all the technological resources at your disposal. Have the leaders of your company or team ever failed to achieve this? Have you ever failed? Perhaps you are wondering if failure really is part of success, if failure is part of learning to hope.

One of the most freeing business books I ever read was *Failing Forward*, by John Maxwell. It encouraged me that indeed, failure is part of success and that winners simply get up more than they are knocked down. You have probably heard that Walt Disney went bankrupt several times before he scored big, that Abraham Lincoln failed as a military leader, that many millionaires have dropped-out of college. Failure is not a permanent state; it is part of the journey. Lately there is great emphasis on the "learning organization" because many companies fear failure and do not know how to learn from it.

Too many business leaders "begin with the end in mind" but they lose perspective in the process from here to there. "Change management" or "change leadership" is about both. Hope is a means-ends continuum. Hope is a journey and a destination. If you are focused on one and not the other, you might be successful but you will probably end up in despair. For example, CEOs or employees who wait for their company to make its IPO and then plan to get out, are not dealers in hope. There are great rewards at the end of hard work, but the journey from here to-there is also full of sweet moments. People who take short cuts to leading change because they want quick results will actually find themselves in another cycle system of disappointment and despair. Only by taking the long way can leaders shape culture and make significant changes.

Destiny is in the Name

If Moses had worked for a trucking company people probably would have called him Mo. In Biblical times a name often had tremendous meaning and 'Mo' would not have conveyed his true persona. Names signified identity and possibly a destiny. Moses actually means "drawn out of the water," as he was found floating down the river and rescued by an Egyptian princess. It is not quite as dynamic a name as Geronimo, Sitting Bull, or Crazy Horse, perhaps, but it is quite significant. He would be a floater and a drifter for many years, but that was not his destiny. The princess probably recognized him as a gift of the gods, as his name could also mean, "son of water."

The name Ramases (one of the Pharaohs) means son of Ra. The M-S-S letters found in both Rameses and Moses' names are part of the root word that means 'son of.' Interestingly, Moses' destiny would be linked to water, to two rivers, the Red Sea and the Jordan. One was a threshold of success, the other an obstacle symbolizing failure. Both bodies of water subsided so the Israelites could continue their journey, marking a new beginning for two different generations, but Moses passed through only one.

If you have seen the Prince of Egypt or read the historic account, then you know that the Egyptian Royal family adopted the Jewish boy Moses. He lived in opulence while the Jewish people lived as slaves. As many young people often do when they cannot reconcile the injustice in the world with their idealism, Moses became an activist. He murdered a guard who was beating one of his people. At this moment Moses faced an identity crisis. An evil act had defined him. He had never been truly Jewish and now he was no longer an Egyptian.

The Pharaoh tried to kill him for his betrayal. Moses ran and hid among the Midianites, a people who lived in what is now the country Jordan, just north of Saudi Arabia. He stumbled upon a group of women "drawing water" from the well who were being harassed by some local shepherds. Moses rescued the women and drove the shepherds away and even "drew water" for the women and fed their flocks. Moses wound up marrying Zipporah, one of the women present at the well. She was devoted to him and followed him on his spiritual quest back to Egypt.

Moses had spent forty years as a shepherd in the desert when Yahweh summoned him to be the leader of the Israelites. He tried to convince God that he was not fit for the task- "Oh Lord, I have never been eloquent, neither in the past nor since you have spoken to your servant. I am slow of speech and tongue," Moses argued.

The dialogue between Moses and God ends with this somewhat comical excuse. Moses tells God that he has never been a good orator, but he clarifies this with "nor since you have spoken to your servant." Just so God knows that the terror of talking with a burning bush was not the only reason for his stammering, Moses added "nor since." Moses had thrown out a bunch of "what if" scenarios to make God rethink his plan, but Yahweh knew how it was going to go down and that Moses could get it done. Moses was not convinced because he still carried with him his false identity. But he set out towards Egypt anyway.

The Pharaoh who wanted Moses dead had himself died and Rameses, Moses' half-brother, had inherited the kingdom. It must have taken considerable courage to return as an outlaw and ask for no small favor as recorded in the book of Exodus- "The God of all gods demands that you let His people go." It is important to understand that the Pharaohs thought of themselves fulfilling that supreme 'God of all gods' role. The Egyptians also believed in and worshiped many lesser gods.

Brilliantly, all the plagues that Yahweh sent were strategically designed to prove that the Egyptian gods paled in comparison. One plague wiped out the livestock and Apis, the sacred bull, could not stop it. One full day of darkness proved the impotence of the sun god Ra. The death of the firstborn, including the death of Pharaoh's son, proved that the king of Egypt was an ordinary mortal being. It took this extreme display of power for Pharaoh to let the slaves go and when they went, the Egyptian people loaded them up with treasure, in an attempt to appease their God.

Moses led the people out of Egypt with their hearts full of hope-fulness but still spiritual infants and in need of being tested. They had not yet come together to imagine, to work as a team, to take any risks, or form a new identity. They were open to a new future, but had not yet discovered authentic hope. This could serve as a lesson to leaders who see positive initial change and yet need to realize that most of the work still lies ahead.

Interestingly, the book of Exodus specifically says that God did not take the short-cut to the Promised Land because that journey would have led to war with the Philistines. "If they face war, they might change their minds and return to Egypt." (Exodus 13:17). The book of Deu-teronomy records that God wanted to take them through the desert where He could test them, to see what was in their hearts. Application-everyone, leaders included, must face the tests in order to discover their true identity.

The first test came immediately. The Pharaoh changed his mind and decided that the loss of labor would be too drastic a change for his nation's economy. With his army behind him, Pharaoh pursued Moses and the Israelites. Two million people were pinned between the water's edge of the Red Sea and the edge of their enemy's sword. Progress seemed impossible when Yahweh commanded Moses to stretch out his staff and part the waters. All of the slaves crossed on dry land and at daybreak the waters flowed back and drowned the Egyptians. Moses was "drawn out of the water" once again and he assumed his new iden-tity as the leader of a free nation. This is success, significance, and quite a surprise finale, I would say.

The Journey

Fast forward a few hundred years to life in the Promised Land after the reign of King David, King Solomon and the many kings after them- most of whom were terrible leaders. God decided to put an end to the corruption and injustice that plagued Jewish society. Right before the Israelites were to go into exile into Babylon, the prophet Micah reminded them of their story, of their hope- "Remember your journey from Shittim to Gilgal." The Jewish God is into journeys, into walking with His people. Genesis records that Yahweh would show up in the Garden of Eden to walk with Adam in the "cool of the day." There is something very significant about a journey, about the process, about the means to an end.

The Israelite journey actually started way back in Egypt but that is considered stage one, from Goshen of Egypt, to Mt. Sinai where Moses received the Ten Commandments. Shittim was the last stop before crossing over to Canaan, to the Promised Land.

Shittim is on the opposite side of the Jordan River across from Canaan. This is close to where Moses left the Israelites and walked up Mount Nevo to die. In the wilderness between Sinai and Shittim the Israelites were tested. They failed the test many times over and finally God made a declaration: The slave generation would not be allowed to enter the Promised Land.

The new generation that grew up in the wilderness had to wait forty years for everyone who came out of Egypt to die and then Joshua led them across the river to Gilgal, the first resting place in the Promised Land. I imagine that wandering in the wilderness without purpose and waiting around for people to die could be quite demoralizing. At

Shittim they pitched their tents one last time on the shore of success. But Shittim marks the last place of shame, the place where God judged His people and purified them once more.

Perhaps in a last ditch-effort to enjoy "the now," and with the knowledge that many would not inherit the Promised Land, despair gave way to decadence. The tragedy began when a neighboring people enticed the Israelites and the "men began to indulge in sexual immorality with Moabite women who invited them to make sacrifices to their gods." (Numbers 25:1-2). Why would they do something that could sabotage their decades of preparation on the eve of their success, right before crossing over into the much-anticipated Promised Land?

Without hope, people make dumb decisions. The Law Moses had received from Yahweh explicitly said the Israelites could not intermarry let alone worship other gods. As punishment for this betrayal, Yahweh ordered the leaders of the tribes to put to death every man who had engaged in the orgy and sacrifice. In defiance, one Israelite man walked right in front of Moses with a Midianite woman on his arm and into his tent. Though scandalous and rebellious, Moses did nothing. He was compromised.

Moses' wife was a Midianite. Even though he had married her before the Law was given, before Yahweh had set the Israelites apart to give them a new identity, Moses could not judge this evil act. Imagine what his wife Zipporah would have said? So, a young man named Phineas took a spear, marched right into the man's tent and while the couple was having sex, he drove the spear through both of them and into the ground. Jewish history records that God praised and blessed Phineas because he was zealous for the Lord's honor.

The Israelites were not only in Shittim, they were in deep Shit-tim, if you catch my meaning. In addition to the men who were ordered killed, a plague of judgment left 24,000 dead. This tragedy almost de-stroyed the people's morale, their hope for a new life. Interestingly, the town that invited the Israelites to worship their gods was located east of Shittim. Had the Lord not intervened in the orgy, the journey might have headed in the opposite direction than to the Promised Land. The Israel-ites might have been absorbed into a race that no longer exists, or no longer has an identity.

Looking Back

There is something about looking back that the Israelite God detests. Perhaps you have heard of Sodom and Gomorrah, notorious for perversion and evil. When running away from this home, a land God judged as having less than 10 good people in it, Lot's wife looked back and turned into a pillar of salt. Whatever that is, it sounds bad. Concern-ing the Israelites, the promised future is what held hope for the people, not the purposeless future behind them that their neighbors offered. When they were tested, the Israelites often complained, "If only we had died by the Lord's hand in Egypt! There we sat around pots of meat and ate all the food we wanted, but you have brought us out into this desert to starve this entire assembly to death" (Exodus 16:3). Their pre-vious life was predictable and familiar, and therefore preferable, though detestable to a God who hoped for their freedom.

Unlike the holistic perspective that connects the past, the pre-sent and the future, looking back is a mindset that says, "Those were the good ol' days. If things could only get back to the time when..."

If your organization is moving forward, many will offer resistance and look back to the days when life was comfortable. That is why Hernan Cortés burned the ships when he reached the new world, so people would focus on moving forward.

Gilgal was the future and the Jordan River was the threshold. Crossing the line meant there was no going back. It was the point of no return. Even still, some Israelites asked Joshua if they could stay on the eastern side of the river after they performed their duty to wage war against the evil nations God was about to judge. Joshua consented.

Shittim represented the darkest darkness right before the dawn. Had they set out eastward, it could have been the end of what is now a great people. When the prophet Micah said, "Remember your journey from Shittim to Gilgal," he wanted them to recall how God delivered them from shame and death into abundance and life. Micah wanted the Israelites to know, that even though they were going into exile again, God would restore their fortunes.

Moses maintained his focus and hope on top of the mountain as he gazed over the river into the Promised Land. Yet, it must have been disappointing for things to end the way they did at Shittim. How did things get so twisted? Moses had set out with a promise, performed amazing miracles, but then got lost in the journey. He failed to shape culture, to transform the slave mentality and instill a new identity. He failed to lead change.

The Wilderness of Change

Moses did not fail to lead change because of his incompetence. God fired him for giving into his former self, his false identity. I will explain how that happened later. First we must back up and identify where things went wrong, where momentum collapsed.

God had assigned Moses to appoint twelve men, representing each tribe, to go and explore the Promised Land, to see what opportunities and threats lay ahead. They returned with two different perspectives, one of despair, one of hope. Ten leaders declared that there were giants in the land who posed a terrible threat. Two dealers in hope agreed that giants did walk the land but insisted that God was bigger and big enough to finish the journey He had started with His people. They focused instead on the giant grapes the land produced.

The Israelites accepted the bad report and began to grumble, suggesting it would be better to return to Egypt. Yahweh warned Moses that He was going to wipe out all of the people who doubted but Moses pleaded with God to forgive them once again. The Lord granted mercy but declared that no one twenty years or older who had seen the miraculous signs in Egypt would be allowed to enter the Promised Land. The two dealers in hope were the only exceptions one of which was Joshua, Moses' successor.

Joshua knew there was more to life than what Egypt had to offer. He wanted an alternative reality, a new beginning, a chance to be free. With visions of vineyards and a land flowing with milk and honey, the younger generation followed Joshua to Gilgal.

Moses did not lead them there but he probably had a hand in preparing them. Had Moses chosen to walk out his destiny, he might have been qualified to lead a hopeful people who possessed a new paradigm for life. Perhaps his frustration with the "stubborn and stiff-necked people," as God nicknamed them, overwhelmed him and he lost confidence in his ability to lead. When put to the test, Moses faltered and his mistake changed his destiny.

While wandering the desert, the Israelites often became thirsty and they complained non-stop. At one point God told Moses to *strike* a nearby rock with his staff and water poured out of it. The same scenario occurred again a bit further in the journey but this time God asked Moses to *speak* to the rock. "So Moses took the staff from the LORD's presence, just as he commanded him. He and Aaron gathered the assembly together in front of the rock and Moses said to them, 'Listen, you rebels, must we bring you water out of this rock?' Then Moses raised his arm and *struck* the rock twice with his staff. Water gushed out, and the community and their livestock drank." (Numbers 20:9-11). Instead of *speaking* to the rock Moses *struck* it.

Two things happened in this defining moment. One- Moses was tested where he was weak, in his communication skills. Many leaders fear that people will not listen to their words and they think that the only way to persuade is to display anger or overpower with huffing and puffing. Two- Moses gave into his weakness at a very symbolic place. Once again, a place of water distinctly marked his life.

Instead of acting like the son of water, as one who could harness power, Moses succumbed to his emotions and let his anger control him. Instead of demonstrating faith, he showed fear. He forced things and tried to control change rather than harness it. Then God said, "Because you did not trust in me enough to honor me as holy in the sight of the Israelites, you will not bring this community into the land I give them" (Numbers 20:12). Not only was Moses acting in his false identity, he was not portraying God's true identity either, that God is trustworthy.

Things Fall Apart

Change is hard because it often goes against human nature. Leaders must remember Newton's law: an object at rest tends to stay at rest until an object acts upon it. Similarly, an object in motion tends to stay in motion until acted upon. These laws teach us that a leader is sometimes required to redirect followers who are moving in the wrong direction and to kick-start those who aren't moving at all.

People resist change for various reasons. Some people refuse to change because they are too comfortable. Others simply do not have the courage to embrace a new identity and take the steps necessary to walk into their destiny. A few lack the wisdom to know how to change but this is usually because they are trying to walk the path alone. The slave generation could not be convinced that they belonged anywhere except in Egypt, no matter how enticing the vision of the promise. Sometimes leaders have to accept that the conditions surrounding them block them from leading change. They can either wait things out, like for an entire generation to die, or move on to another, more favorable environment where they can lead.

Moses was stuck with stubborn people, for better, for worse. It is important to realize, though, that a greater failure would have been to let the Israelites perish in the wilderness and cease to exist altogether. Moses assumed the role of manager when the conditions made it almost impossible for him to lead. He succeeded at preserving the people. In some ways he is like Ernest Shakleton, who failed to cross Antarctica but pulled off probably the greatest rescue of recorded modern history. Sometimes leadership is simply about survival, about weathering the storm.

The question is, "What do you have to work with?" "What are the conditions like- favorable towards leadership or more of a hostile environment to change?" Before you come to conclusions too quickly and give up on your team too early, let's examine the hope diamond briefly in relation to Moses and the Israelites. Let's look for clues to your own leadership dynamic. The last chapter will walk you through how to lead change and shape culture using this hope paradigm. Your new hope knowledge merits at least one experiment to initiate change, build momentum, and see things through, as much as it depends on you. You might not feel hopeful right now, but I've come to realize that at times like that is when hope often finds me.

Hopeful vs. Hope

The hope journey starts with adversity and the Israelites had plenty of it living in Egypt. They cried out to God in one voice and Yahweh responded by sending Moses to deliver them out of slavery. Moses came to fulfill a promise made long ago to Abraham- to give the Israelites their own land. Moses used vivid descriptions to help the people imagine an alternative reality- the Promised Land was "a land flowing with milk and honey." Though hopeful when they left Egypt, the Israelites quickly lost heart when they faced new challenges. They were forced to work as a team and take risks, like crossing the Red Sea, but they never owned the process. They never identified with God, Moses, or their new destiny.

The Israelites stopped imagining because they had an identity issue. Free people are free to imagine. Slaves accept reality as it is and the Israelites had been accepting it for over 400 years. Moses painted a crystal clear vision but the people could not see it. They kept rehearsing the familiar images of their life in Egypt. This is where the hope diamond dissolves. If people do not take risks when hopefulness is high, hope will shut down quickly.

The Israelites never discovered hope because they never found a new identity. A new logo or mission statement would not solve this deeply rooted problem. Dress-down Fridays and motivational speakers would not be enough to boost morale. Without an identity linking the individual to the team- to the organization, hope shuts down. Freedom for freedom sake is not enough to inspire hope. There must be a purpose a free people can pursue.

There will always be high turnover in business as long as there are jobs people perceive as purposeless or insignificant, a job anyone can fill. Once the Israelites decided not to enter the Promised Land, the purpose freedom afforded disappeared. Moses failed because of poor leadership conditions. Accept this truth. This might be a hard pill to swallow, especially if you are an American, taught to pull yourself up by your bootstraps and make things happen. Face it, there are some people a leader cannot lead. In regards to this phenomenon one leader I know said, "I can't lead people who don't want to be led. I can't nail jello to the wall either. I can't push a rope either." There are some things a leader cannot do.

I hope this truth relieves you of a burden that is not yours to carry. It might mean you get fired from your job but so will the next leader after you. When I worked as a hotel supervisor, there were eleven Front Desk Managers in three years. The one who left while I was there recognized early on that this particular hotel was not a leader-friendly environment. They took a better job elsewhere and I assumed the position temporarily. I found out the same thing and I moved on within a few months. This is life. This is reality. Accept it and move on or, if you love the organization enough, stick in there until the conditions change.

That's right, sometimes change happens without you and you have to simply wait for it. It could take a lifetime to lead change and shape culture. It could take many generations to fulfill what you start out to do. This is not failure, just because you did not get it done in your few short days on this planet. Jamie Clark, an "adventure-preneur" that attempted Mt. Everest three times before he reached the summit, said, "If you're not doing something that *cannot* be accomplished in your life-time, your vision is too small." Some leaders are before their time but that does not make them failures, just unappreciated. Like Moses, set your sights on the promising future even as termination or death approaches.

In whatever mountain you face, if things do not look hopeful, you can still embrace the hope paradigm for change. Interestingly, the Bible makes a promise that those who hope will not be disappointed. I have yet to prove that false in my own life. There are times when I lose heart and get discouraged, but I keep working with teams and I keep taking risks because I know that just around the corner something is going to pop-up and things will turn out better than I could have imagined. I struggle with you. I encourage you to put one foot in front of the other and we will reach the summit too.

Age ??

Dealer in Hope

Leading change and shaping culture:

What change is it you are trying to create? Describe what

the new reality will look like.

_____

_____

_____

_____

In the classic Count of Monte Cristo, Alexander Dumas tells the story of Edmond Dantes. This blissful young man has everything going for him, just promoted to captain of a ship and celebrating with his fiancé on the eve of their wedding. Then his destiny is altered. Conspirators frame Dantes who is thus charged with treason for supporting the usurper Napoleon Bonaparte. He is sent to the Chateau d' If, a prison on an island from which there is no reasonable escape, where he will serve a life sentence.

After thirteen years Dantes finally escapes, though not in the form he had been pursuing all those years. His inmate and mentor reveals the location of a hidden treasure which empowers Dantes to assume his new identity as the Count of Monte Cristo when he returns to the world.

No one recognizes a man who was supposed to be dead and the Count works mischievously to upend the status quo and bring all the conspirators to justice. In so doing, Dantes restores the fortunes of his friends who had suffered and lost much due to the "powers that be." It is a tale of hope.

Many mistake the major theme of the story as revenge. Alexander Dumas had something else in mind, though, as the last page of his tale reveals: "Live then, and be happy, beloved children of my heart, and never forget that until the day when God will deign to reveal the future to man, all human wisdom is contained in these two words, Wait and Hope. Your friend, Edmond Dantes, Count of Monte Cristo." A closer look at this epic novel echoes what I've been saying throughout this book about hope. All the elements are there- suffering, voice, promises, imagination, team work, risk taking, and a new identity. In sustaining hope, Dantes is able to create a new and better reality for his friends and for himself. I hope the same for you and your organization.

This chapter is a practical step-by-step guide for implementing the hope paradigm to lead change and shape culture. I understand that every context is different, of course, but the hope diamond is a universal framework. I promise you will not be disappointed if you apply what you already know about some of the steps and walk through the whole process (without taking short cuts).

Step #1 Take the Hope Assessment

I recommend that you assess your environment before you experiment with the hope paradigm. The hopescape assessment is in the appendices and you may make as many copies as you like. There is a key to help you interpret the results and determine leverage points to create a hope environment. Without a hopescape, any change you initiate will face greater resistance or be impossible to achieve.

Step #2 Practice Systems Thinking

The hopescape assessment evaluates your organization in each of the six elements: voice, promises, imagination, team work, risk taking, and identity. It is important to keep in mind that four of these elements are linked together in a feedback loop. Where hope increases, the other four elements in the hope diamond increase too.

Remember, the hope diamond is not a closed system. For example, risk taking may be low in your organization, but a leader could inject a new promise that inspires imagination and team work and, BOOM- risk taking spikes again. Other outside variables affect team work which could indirectly affect the other hope elements.

If you discover that your organization is weak in taking risks, do not act on this insight too early. Telling people to take more risks will probably not restore hope or achieve success. Walk through the entire hope paradigm. Even though taking risks might seem like a leverage point, the breakdown could actually lie with promises or imagination. People have a hard time walking into something blindly. Taking action when the stakes are high requires clarity of vision. If the vision is clear but leadership has not given a stamp of approval (a promise to back-up the team with resources) then risk taking will naturally be lower. It is essential to grasp the whole system when leading change.

Step #3 Pinch Your People

Sometimes a leader perceives a necessary change that the people in the organization do not. They might be comfortable where they are and not voicing a need for change. It is the responsibility of the leader to clarify the needed change but, before that, to help people understand the problem, the reason for change. The leader pinches people to wake them from their slumber. It is important for the organization to reach a frustration point, for the people to express their voice and discover a desire for change.

Most leaders want to begin with a great vision that inspires others, but that leader will find polite approval more than committed stakeholders. A vision paints a picture of an alternative reality that must be compared to the unwanted future. People may be comfortable now but they must be made to see how fleeting that luxury is. I do not recommend threatening people with losing their job, however, as that destroys hope and produces fear.

The promise a leader makes is not, "We will all be out of a job if we don't..." That is not a promise; it is a negative idea about the future. The negative must be addressed and faced head-on but it must be coupled with the wonderful, fantastic, amazing alternative reality towards which you are leading the people. Remember this metaphor- you are in the desert but you are leading people to an oasis. The two are coupled: adversity and vision. Problem and solution. Pain and gain.

Step #4 Define the Change You Want

Remove the words "better," "more," "improved," and other buzz words like "next level" from your vision pitch. Saying you want "more sales" or "better customer service," or that you want to take your organization to the "next level" is absolutely void of power and persuasion. Unfortunately the corporate world took vision and reduced it to an elevator speech which has poorly molded most leaders' visionary skills. Yeah, it's nice to impress people with a concise purpose, but vision is meant to be dynamic.

The key distinction you will encounter in a good vision pitch is rare these days. It is not what you say; it is what people see- thus the word vision. However, most vision statements are too wordy, too boring, too vague, and too generic. Lame tag-lines include:

"To outperform our competitors."

"To be the best in our class."

"To be the number one global provider."

These are grandiose words masked in unoriginality and communicate nothing. If a phrase or sentence sears an image in your mind, then that is a good vision statement. Create vivid pictures with your words. Most people think a vision statement communicates a good idea. NO. A good vision statement communicates an unforgettable image.

Read most Fortune 500 vision statements and ask yourself if they communicate an idea or an image. For example, the word "freedom" is an idea. The phrase "Break the chains off my bones!" creates an image. Though often crass, Bon Jovi is a master at word pictures. A lyric line in his song *Bed of Roses* says, "I wake up and french kiss the morning." This follows an experience most people have had at one time

161

or another- going to bed drunk and waking up with a hangover. If a CEO had written the song, he might have said, "I wake up in the morning and I'm dehydrated."

Images are more powerful than ideas.

Blaze of Glory is another song that captures the imagination:

> "I wake up in the morning and I raise my weary head. I got an old coat for a pillow and the earth was last night's bed. I don't know where I'm going, only God knows where I've been. I'm a devil on the run, a six gun lover, a candle in the wind."

Could your vision, your change initiative, be a line in a song, a title to a novel? A vision pitch is a mini-story. It should make the reader want to know how it's going to end. Sadly, I usually want a company's vision statement to end before I finish reading it, they are so bad. Most stories have a variety of characters who experience life from a different perspective. So should there exist a variety of vision statements in the life of an organization. Executives want employees to be passionate about their fresh idea they formulated during a weekend retreat which ossified before they even returned to the office. Instead, give your employees a theme and let them invent images to express it. Create a hundred vision statements. People will own their image more anyway than anything force-fed.

Any change you want to lead must be expressed creatively and concisely, with as much attention as if you were formulating a vision statement. Get your people to echo the vision in their own words. At first they might voice negative statements rather than use positive words to communicate the vision. Help them spin it to harness positive energy rather than express negative emotion. This is the step from voice to imagination. For example, if you are trying to improve employee interactions- instead of saying, "Don't shame or blame" (an *idea* stated in the negative), the same vision can be communicated as a positive *image*- "Put a pretty dress on the people mess." In other words, give people the benefit of the doubt and make them look good.

Visionary leaders have ten ways to say the same thing, they just use different images to grab people's attention. A vision is organic, constantly changing yet powerfully consistent. In order to lead change or shape culture, our words have to communicate what we want. People cannot read our minds. When it comes to pitching change, show it when you say it.

Step #5 Make Promises You Can Keep

The previous four steps helped create a hopescape. By now you should be able to clearly articulate the frustrations your people feel, whether natural or from your instigations. The time is ripe to make a few promises you can definitely keep.

Promises must be
1. *specific* yet *broad*
2. *timely*
3. not create *dependence* on the leader
4. communicate *shared destiny*.

Remember, "No action" is almost synonymous with a broken promise- time being the only differentiator. Be careful with the promises you make because they will make or break you. How does the following example *promise* achieve all four criteria I have suggested?

"We need to figure out a system to get clients their orders one day earlier. If we can achieve 80% on-time delivery over the next full month, everyone will be awarded a three-day weekend at the Riverside Hilton the following week. We're interested in your rest after putting forth extra effort. I have told my softball team I can't play these next two weeks and my family understands I need to be focused at work right now. I will put in the necessary hours to make sure I can offer you the support we need to succeed. We need more than compliance on this one. We need focused commitment. Can the team count on you? (Get a verbal yes from people and ask them to express what sacrifices they will have to make to lead this change- this will help people bond more as a team). Then ask the imagination question- What do we need to do to create this delivery system?"

The promise is specific because it includes a tangible incentive- three-day weekend at the Riverside Hotel. It is broad because the leader says, "I will put in the necessary hours to make sure I can offer you the support we need to succeed." Yet, the rhetoric emphasizes "we," not "I," so the team knows the leader is not doing all the work.

This prevents dependence. The fulfillment of this promise goes into effect almost immediately and the reward is within the near future. The promise is therefore timely. By expressing what sacrifices everyone will have to make, the leader creates an awareness of a shared destiny.

If the leader does not show-up early and stay late at work, If the leader does not demonstrate more interest in the team and communicate more than usual, if the leader does not make sure the employees get rest, even if they miss the target, then the people will lose hope that the leader can fulfill promises. Yes, I wrote "even if they miss the target" they should earn rest. They might not earn the three-day weekend retreat but a day-off is important. This must be factored in with your promise and supported by the organization. You don't explicitly promise a free day-off if the team misses the target, as there should be no incentives for failure. However, creating hope takes time and sometimes failure is part of the process. Prove that leadership Is full of good surprises and the next time you lead change, your team will be willing to make even more sacrifices to succeed.

Step #6 Let Imaginations Run Wild

The number one rule of any brainstorm session is do not critique. Make room for every idea and write them all down. If you skip someone, make sure their idea is captured by a previous thought. Verbally communicate how the idea connects so the person does not feel slighted (an instant brainstorm-energy killer). Other etiquette must be observed as well, like making sure everyone has an opportunity to talk and one person does not generate all the ideas. Do not allow for "dittos" or other confirmations which seal the deal too early.

Everyone must contribute one idea of their own. Jumping on any one specific idea too early, even though it might seem obvious at the time, could short-circuit the project if progress dead-ends along the way. The idea that initially seemed right might flat-line and another person's brainstorm might be more appropriate given new conditions that emerged. The more ideas the merrier. Be ridiculous, almost ludicrous. Give an award for the zaniest, yet relevant idea. Then it is time to whittle things down and tame the imagination.

For the short-term change initiatives there are a variety of tools and approaches to achieve the same result. If you want to implement an innovation system that spurs the imagination on a regular basis, with the long-term in view, I have included a tool you can adapt for your situation.

For immediate problem-solving, backcasting is a proven approach to innovation. It is similar to reverse engineering. In step four you clearly articulated the change your team wants to see in effect. Backcasting starts with the end vision and works backwards. What is one step before the finished outcome?

In the example of a faster delivery system, the end result is a customer with a smile on their face because they have a box in their hand delivered by FedEx or UPS one day earlier than expected. What happened before that? The UPS man got into his truck, left the hub and drove his daily route. What happened before that? Keep asking that question until you narrow down your search for the log-jam. Do you need another manufacturing facility that is closer to the majority of your customers? That is a long-term solution. What is a short-term solution?

The backcasting process is quite simple but quite detailed. Many technologies have been invented simply in the process to achieve another more sophisticated technology. It happened in the process, usually from a backcasting exercise.

If you have the long-term in mind, I suggest a simple innovation/ idea funnel. The funnel flows from red to green. Green is an idea that has won the support of many and which the organization should seriously consider.

The $1,000,000 Experiment

ideas -- tagged -- supported -- improved -- sponsored

Red- Every idea is listed.

Orange- Peers can *tag* the idea with clarification questions or smiley faces.

Yellow- Peers can *support* the idea by offering practical application or "why it would work" info.

Light green- Peers can *improve* on the idea by altering one aspect of it.

Green- Once an idea is improved upon, is merited by a leader, passes other rigorous innovation evaluations, the company will *sponsor* it.

If the idea proves profitable, all people involved in the process will receive back equal portion of the first million dollars profit (or any size profits depending on the size of your organization and the impact of the innovation). Bono of U2 said, "If you didn't believe the impossible was possible, you'd never get anywhere." When people imagine great things, they soon realize that it is impossible to achieve them alone. Team work is absolutely necessary to go from impossible to possible.

Step #7 Spend Yourself

Teddy Roosevelt said, "...the credit belongs to the man who spends himself in a worth cause." I want to spin his words slightly and encourage you to "spend" yourself- meaning, realize that what you are doing requires more than 100% of what you can give. Come to the end of yourself and be dependent on a team. It is risky to trust others, but you cannot find hope without spending yourself and realizing you're still short on the bill. Sometimes this is more difficult than others, depending on the people who surround you, but in the end it will be worth it.

As a team leader you might not have a choice with whom you work; you might have to "work with what you got." However, the whole is usually greater than the sum of the parts when it comes to professional work and more than likely your team will collaborate if nothing more than as a strategic alliance to achieve the imagined goal. This goal is your common thread, your constant in the middle of chaos. But you must come back to the dream and re-visit the vision constantly as new obstacles arise.

NASA

My friend, whom I will call Steve, is an engineer at NASA and has been working on a pet project for the last two years. This is work in addition to what is laid out in his job description and which he is pursuing as a passion more than for any other reason. He has been constantly barraged with obstacles and often distracted by conflicting schedules. On top of this, Steve's father has been on death's door for almost a year and Steve has traveled hundreds of miles every month, sometimes taking weeks off work, to care for his dad.

Steve confessed to me that he had reached the end of himself. He was emotionally spent and had nothing left to give. His work load kept piling up, hundreds of emails to return every day, and progress to maintain even while away from the office. In the midst of chaos Steve found himself surrounded by a fantastic team. Steve's father had attended a local church and when he fell ill, the pastor and congregation rose to the occasion. Even the nursing staff at the hospital went out of their way to make sure Steve's father received the best care and they never quit fighting with his dad who refused to die.

When back home in Virginia, Steve performed his normal duties with his usual team of engineers. This routine was frequently interrupted by his pet project, which required numerous visits to Seattle, Washington. Steve had brokered a deal between Boeing, NASA and other minor players in a strategic alliance to reduce jet engine noise. It doesn't sound fancy but innovation isn't always glamorous. This one change- simply making jets quieter, could greatly impact real estate, residential construction, retail, and other industries within a community.

Steve is leading change through team work in every area of his life. By "spend yourself" I mean don't go it alone. Significant change is not a "one man show," so don't pretend it is. Rely on your teammates. Empower them. Help them keep in mind the big picture of which individuals often lose sight when they concentrate on one specific area of a project. What they are doing is important but not as important as what will be produced when all the pieces of the puzzle are put together.

In the process of working together, your role as the leader is to practice strategic foresight. Help your team to identify potential obstacles and create proper solutions. With foresight you can encourage your team to take risks because you can envision the rewards to come.

Step #8 Bet the Farm

Leading change might require convincing the board to invest 20% more in R&D. This is a huge risk. Marketing is another risk, especially for small businesses that could fold if their dollars do not yield immediate results. You might realize that hiring a new employee could stretch the budget but without their expertise new streams of revenue will be difficult to generate. Risks surround leaders.

This is a touchy subject because many companies pride themselves in risk aversion. Forecast analysts are hired to predict within a few percentage points how well the company is expected to perform. Forecasting sales has become a science and sales figures impact decision-making probably more than any other business variable.

Companies forget how much risk they took to become the successful organization they are today. The stakes get too high and they ease off the accelerator. Leaders have to challenge this inertia and emphasize to other decision-makers what the next level of success will require. Leaders want to stretch and grow, face new challenges and overcome obstacles. That is why those who seem to have arrived at the prize and are making six or seven figures will leave their secure position at a mature company to tackle the unknown in a smaller upstart that can't pay them half as much.

Step #9 Symbolize to Identify

Batman wanted to change the world and put an end to corruption in his city. "I can't do that as Bruce Wayne, as a man... But as a symbol I can be incorruptible," he tells his butler Alfred. Somehow, some way, as a dealer in hope, any significant change you lead must be symbolic. For decades Fidel Castro milked the martyrdom of Che Guevara, the symbol of the Cuban Revolution. Religions use symbols and icons to encapsulate the purpose and meaning for their cause. Brands try to accomplish the same thing- to get people to identify and be loyal to their company.

Only significant change requires a symbol. Creating a faster delivery system does not make people's hearts beat faster or inspire new songs. But fighting cancer does. People identify with Lance Armstrong not only because he fought cancer and won but because he strives and even surpasses the efforts of healthier people who compete against him in cycling. He gave people a small symbol to wear, a little yellow bracelet, with the words "Live Strong" and over 50 million sold worldwide within the first year. It was a craze that later turned into a fashion fad that everyone claimed and used as a stamp for their cause. Saturation couldn't even destroy this symbol because the die-hards still wear the yellow band.

Like a vision, symbols must be dynamic and evolve. A new symbol has to rise up. I just saw a commercial put on by Nike and Live Strong called "Scream Hope." Sean Swarner, the first cancer survivor to summit Mt. Everest, screams "Hope" from the "highest platform" in the world. Find your platform to scream from.

The change you lead might seem insignificant but you must re-imagine what it is you are doing. Two guys working side by side were both asked what they were doing. One said, "I'm laying brick." The other said, "I'm building a home." You must connect the simple, seemingly mundane, to the magnificent whole.

I mentioned earlier that my friend Chris, who is a black belt in Six Sigma management, took a promotion without the $30,000 pay increase that the company could not afford. He is like Ishmael, the only survivor in the tale Moby Dick. Ishmael said, "But I am one of those who never take on about princely fortunes, and am quite content if the world is ready to board and lodge me, while I am putting up at this grim sign of the Thunder Cloud." Chris does what he does because he identifies with something bigger than himself. As a Christian, Chris identifies with Jesus Christ and this compels him to make sacrifices as Jesus did. He works in the hope that he can be part of something that exceeds his imagination and where his actions will echo in eternity.

You might identify with a religious leader, an historic figure, or a great man or woman like your father/ mother or mentor. Leaders identify with successful and significant people. If your team or your organization is to discover hope and work in hope, you must help them identify with the stuff of legends. Work is part of their story and it must be epic, not tragic. You are not the author of their story but your presence and dialogue creates a purposeful relationship.

Speaking practically, if you do not possess the power and perspective of hope for the work you do, it will be impossible to help others discover purpose and identify with those who came before them. Dealers in hope know their organization's history, how the founders struggled and overcame the impossible. These leaders talk about the great things people have done through the years to make the organization great. They admit the faults and shortcomings and realize that some had to fail so others could succeed. You must let your work become who you are, not just what you do. If you cannot do that, you are in the wrong profession. Get out while you still can. Sync with your work and identify with those who inspire you.

Symbolizing the change you want to create takes work. Be original and creative. Pictures are one form of expression. Art is better than a logo, though, because it is one of a kind and therefore possesses intrinsic authenticity.

On the internet Google will often transform their name-logo by fashioning it to suit different themes or holidays. On the anniversary of the moon landing they sculpted their name using moon craters. This keeps their image fresh. Also, in so doing, they identified with the great astronauts who took one small step, yet one giant step for humankind. Constantly create and add to your company's story so people can identify and discover hope.

Step #10 Keep Hope Alive

If you walked through the other nine steps, you most likely discovered hope. You wake up in the morning slightly more confident about your work and ready to face the challenges of the day. But a challenge might arise that is bigger than the hope you currently hold. Use the hope you have to fuel your team's imagination, risk taking, and identity once again. You will cycle through the hope diamond a few times before a significant change is realized.

Do not be discouraged if your team has less hope than you. Leaders usually walk through the process diligently but followers get distracted. Teach them the hope paradigm and have them take the hope assessment too. If you keep working through this hope process in all areas of your life, you will develop what Shade calls "habits of hope." This is a powerful maturity that others might observe as humble confidence or "having your act together" but you will know it is the power of hope working in your life. Dr. Groopman's research shows that cancer patients who demonstrated hope recovered more often than those without it. It is a game changer, a life changer.

If you want to be a dealer in hope, to lead change and shape culture for a better future reality, keep hope alive. Remember, hope is an orientation and action towards the most meaningful future. "Live then, and be happy, beloved children of my heart, and never forget that until the day when God deigns to reveal the future to man, all human wisdom is contained in these two words, Wait and Hope."

– The Count of Monte Cristo

Appendix

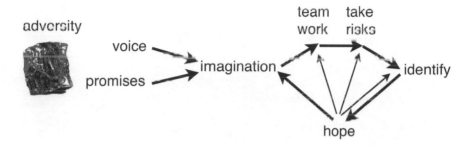

Hopescape Assessment

The audit is designed to assess you and your company's hope level and potential in a number of different ways. Each question consists of two bipolar parts: a primary statement and a counter or opposite statement. You are to see which of the two statements most closely describes you. Neither statement may *exactly* describe your attitudes or actions, but choose the one that is the closest fit to you. Do not try to think of what would be the 'best' answer; simply answer honestly how you view yourself against these statements. There are five blocks for each question and you should choose the **ONE** that most closely reflects the statement you preferred. For example:

Statement	Very true	Somewhat true	50-50	Somewhat true	Very True	Counter Statement
0/ I like active holidays.		X				0/ I like quiet, restful, holidays.

1/ I feel I can be honest with co-workers (team members) about problems at work.			1/ I feel I have to guard what I say around most people.
2/ I hear people complain about policies and procedures.			2/ I notice people take formal complaints to their supervisors.
3/ The supervisor shares company problems with the team.			3/ The supervisor is closed-mouthed about certain issues.
4/ I stick to the way I know my boss wants things done.			4/ I think of new ways to solve problems all the time.
5/ I notice people gather informally to talk about new ideas.			5/ It seems that my team doesn't interact much voluntarily.
6/ Formal brainstorm meetings are usually one person talking.			6/ I feel comfortable sharing ideas in formal meetings.
7/ People withhold information from others on the same team.			7/ People on the same team communicate thoroughly.
8/ The supervisor is difficult to work with.			8/ The supervisor is approachable.
9/ I rather work on a team than by myself.			9/ I prefer to work alone on most projects.
10/ I couldn't tell you the history of my company.			10/ My company's history is very interesting.
11/ I am proud of and sometimes brag about where I work.			11/ I never talk about where I work after work hours.
12/ I don't mind making sacrifices at work when times are tough.			12/ I don't see why employees should work overtime without compensation.

13/ Risk taking is looked down on.					13/ Employees are encouraged to take risks.
14/ I take risks often.					14/ I keep to what is proven and expected.
15/ I am encouraged and given time to work on pet projects.					15/ There is little time to pursue creative ideas.
16/ The company often delays keeping their promises.					16/ The company always follows through on their promises.
17/ The company makes sacrifices to ensure deadlines are met.					17/ Deadlines are not strictly adhered to.
18/ I do not have specific goals written down.					18/ I clearly define my goals and accomplish them by the date I set.
19/ I meet my goals earlier than expected.					19/ I sometimes make excuses for not reaching my goals on time.
20/ My team looks for shortcuts to get the project done.					20/ My team looks for ways to go the extra mile.
21/ Our department makes sure to spend our whole budget.					21/ Our department tries to avoid spending the entire budget.
22/ I look forward to going to work everyday					22/ I am often bored at work.

Every question is graded on a scale of odd numbers from 1-9.

1, 3, 5, 7, 9 are the possible scores for each answer. The middle box on the test always scores a 5. 1 is the lowest and 9 is the highest. The square around the phrases below indicates which is the "hope" answer and will score a 9 if marked "very true" on the assessment.

Voice

1. | I feel that I can be honest with my team about problems at work |

I feel that I have to guard what I say around most people

2. I hear people complain about policies and procedures

| I notice people take formal complaints to their supervisors |

3. | The supervisor shares company problems with the team |

The supervisor is closed mouthed about certain issues

Imagine

4. | I think of new ways to solve problems all the time |

I stick to the way I know my boss wants things done

5. | I notice people gather informally to talk about new ideas |

It seems that my team doesn't interact much voluntarily

6. formal brainstorm meetings are usually one person talking

| I feel comfortable contributing ideas in formal brainstorm meetings |

Teamwork

7. people withhold information from others on the same team

| people on the same team communicate thoroughly |

8. | the project manager is approachable |

the project manager is difficult to work with

9. | I rather work on a team than by myself |

I prefer to work alone on most projects

Identify

10. | my company's history is very interesting |

I couldn't tell you the history of my company

11. | I am proud of and brag about where I work |

I never talk about where I work after work hours

12. | I don't mind making sacrifices when times are tough |

I don't see why employees should work overtime without compensation

Take Risks

13. Risk taking is looked down upon

| Employees are encouraged to take risks |

14. | I take risks often |

I keep to what is proven and expected

15. | I am encouraged and given time to work on pet projects |

There is little time to pursue creative ideas

Promise

16. | The company always follows through on their promises to their employees |

The company often delays keeping their promises

17. | The company makes sacrifices to ensure deadlines are met |

Deadlines are not strictly adhered to

18. I do not have specific goals written down

| I clearly define my goals and accomplish them by the date I set |

Surprise

19. | I meet my goals earlier than expected |

I make excuses for not reaching my goals on time

20. | my team looks for ways to go the extra mile |

my team looks for short-cuts to get the project done

21. our department makes sure to spend the whole annual budget

| our department tries to avoid spending the entire budget |

22. Last question- joy, or satisfaction, is the obvious fruit of hope. If an employee dreads going to work in the morning, if their favorite saying is "TGI Friday," then they probably need an infusion of hope.
Add up the scores from each question. Then divide by 198 to get a hopescape index percentage.

Bibliography

1999, The Holy Bible, New International Version

Anderson, 1997, System Thinking Basics

Assayas, 2005, Bono on Bono

Axelrod and Cohen, 1999, Harnessing Complexity

Bishop, 2001, Change Management

Brueggemann, 1986, Hopeful Imagination

Canton, 2006, The Extreme Future

Covey, 1990, 7 Habits of highly effective people

Cruikshank, 2006, The Apple Way

Daft, 2005, The Leadership Experience

Diamond, 1997, Guns, Germs and Steel

Eldredge, 2001, Wild At Heart

Fishman 2007, John Dewey and the phiosophy and practice of hope.

Frankl, 1959, Man's Search for Meaning

Frankl, 1968, Will to meaning

Gladwell, 2000, The Tipping Point

Grant, 1996, Carry A Big Stick

Hines, 2006, The Futurist

Kahney, 2008, Inside Steve's brain

Kahney, 2004, The cult of mac

Kappelman, 2001, Marshall McLuhan: "The medium is the message"

Kauffman, 1980, An Introduction In Systems Thinking

Kouzes, 2003, Credibility

Kuhn, 1970, The Structure of Scientific Revolutions

Maxwell, 1998, 21 Irrefutable Laws of Leadership

Mayra, 2008, An Introduction to game studies

McLaren, 2007, Everything Must Change

Mitchell, 2009, Why Obama Won: the making of a president

Moltmann, 1967, Theology of Hope

Obama, 2006, Audacity of Hope

Plato, The Republic

Polak, 1973, The Image of the Future

Rorty, 1999, Philosophy and social hope

Sabato, 2010, The Year of Obama: How Barak Obama won the...

Senge, 1990, The Fifth Discipline

Shade, 2001, Habits of hope

Snyder, 2000, Handbook of hope

Stout, 2006, Time for a change

Terry, 1993, Authentic Leadership: Courage in action

Tinder, 1999, The fabric of hope

Toffler, 1970, Future Shock

Vicere and Fulmer, 1998, Leadership by design

Wark, 2007, Gamer Theory

Weatherford, 2004, Ghengis Khan and the making of the modern world

Wright, 2008, Surprised by Hope

Young and Simon, 2005, iCon: Steve Jobs, the greatest second act in
     history

Movies that teach about hope.

Terminal- (Tom Hanks & Catherine Zeta Jones)

Shawshank Redemption- (Morgan Freeman)

Stranger than Fiction- (Will Ferrel)

50 First Dates (Adam Sandler & Drew Barrymore)

The Notebook (Ryan Gosling & Rachel McAdams)

The Truman Show (Jim Carrey)

The Count of MonteCristo (James Caviezel)

The Ultimate Gift (Abigail Breslin)

The Family Man (Nicholas Cage & Téa Leoni)

Braveheart (Mel Gibson)

Moulin Rouge (Nicole Kidman & Ewan McGregor)

Goal (Leonardo Guerra)

Amazing Grace (Ioan Gruffudd)

Made in the USA
San Bernardino, CA
20 May 2013